THE DECEPTION WITHIN

A normal family with extraordinary experiences.

A True Story

"*Blessed is the one who perseveres under trial because, having stood the test, that person will receive the crown of life that the Lord has promised to those who love him.*"– James 1:12

THE DECEPTION WITHIN

By: Luz Reyes Luna

Dedication

To my beloved parents Crispin and Remedios Reyes. We are forever in your debt for all the love, patience, understanding, kindness, guidance and support you have given to each of us. Your legacy will continue to flourish in the lives of your grandchildren and great-grandchildren.

My endless thanks to you, my beloved Papa and Mama.

Acknowledgement

To my brother, **Junior**, who played a major role — provided information, reviewed early drafts from beginning to end, offered suggestions on what to include and what I would otherwise have forgotten to include. He guided, encouraged and inspired me from the start, and later brainstormed with me for suitable titles, taglines, cover design and video advert ideas. I could not have finished this book without your help. Thank you very much for your patience and for believing in me.

To my sister, **Teresa**, who helped and contributed information. She gave me the confidence to push through given that English is my second language. I appreciate your encouragement and your faith in me. Thank you very much.

To my husband, **Simon,** who supported me unconditionally throughout the entire process and provided me with everything I needed to publish this book. Thank you very much.

To my editor, **David E. Potts**, who did an excellent job of editing, and made an in-depth analysis of my manuscript, he patiently guided me through the entire process, and suggested the ideal title, which I have adopted. This book would not have been made possible without your help. Working with you was enjoyable and I value your kindness, understanding and commitment. Thank you very much.

To my book and logo designer, **Muhammad Hassan**, who did a superb job, I appreciate your patience, dedication and honesty. Thank you so much.

Table Of Contents

EPISODE 1

THE HUMBLE BEGINNING

Young and Tenacious

"Cast your cares on the LORD and he will sustain you; he will never let the righteous be shaken."–Psalm 55:22

United, a charming and sprightly couple had to tackle countless and unimaginable obstacles in life. Like two giant majestic trees with branches intertwined, they fearlessly faced the beginning of each new day that God gave them. At only eighteen years of age, with little, and soon to have an expanding family of eight, they had to work tirelessly, turning nights into days, burning the midnight oil to a standstill.

Crispin T. Reyes, a conscientious and energetic man, was born in Dinalupihan on May 29, 1916, and Remedios L. Tiangco, a beautiful and demure lady, was born in the city of Balanga on November 7, 1916, both in the Province of Bataan. Bataan is one of the peninsulas in the Philippines and famous for the Bataan Death March of April 9, 1942, during the Japanese occupation of World War II.

It was destined by God that they would cross paths.

One day in school, happily conversing with the other students, with a glow on his charming face, Crispin got bored. He upturned his classmate's chair onto the floor. His startled classmate was lying on his back with his feet waggling up in the air as Crispin laughed uncontrollably, until the teacher intervened and made Crispin sit between the two girls as punishment. While the embarrassed Crispin sat quietly, his keen eyes were drawn to the hands of one girl. They were lovely, shaped like long tapered candles. He was struck by her radiance as he looked at her face and thought, "She looks like an angel." Thus began their enduring love story.

Remedios was the youngest of six children. Childhood came to a screeching halt for her when her mom passed away unexpectedly, she didn't want to return to school. Being the baby of the family, and so attached to her mother, she was inconsolable.

Josefa, Remedios' oldest sister, acted as her mother and decided for her. No matter how many times Josefa advised Remedios to return to school after her mother died, she refused. It took a year until she was finished grieving for her mother. She would have never met Crispin had she not skipped a year of school. God has mysterious ways of working!

Because it was difficult for Josefa to attend to Remedios since she had her own family, she sent her to the Santa Catalina convent so that she could have a good upbringing. Later, Josefa found the arrangement to be difficult, so she encouraged Remedios and Crispin to marry, even though they were not quite ready to be husband and wife. They married in 1934.

Determined, Crispin continued to be busy with school with his meager allowance that was barely enough to support one person, so he left Remedios with his family in Bataan while he studied in Manila. After about a year, Crispin's sister paid him a visit. She advised Crispin to bring his wife to Manila to join him because the family was not treating his wife fairly.

Remedios, feeling helpless and distraught, would cry herself to sleep some nights because of the unfair treatment she received from her sisters-in-law, but she never complained. One day, as she was lying down in bed, uncontrollably sobbing, she heard a man's voice… deep and gentle, coming from nowhere: "My child, do not cry. You will have everything one day and you will need none of them." She felt miraculously uplifted and relieved after hearing this.

Crispin whisked Remedios away to Manila to be with him. He didn't want his family to cause his beloved wife any unnecessary heartache, not even for a minute more; he loved his beautiful wife way too much to make her suffer any longer.

Despite adversity, Crispin finished high school in three years and graduated as valedictorian. He then supported himself by attending the University of the Philippines to study law. While studying at the university he worked as a student assistant. On a meager allowance, he could support Remedios and their first child, Cecilia, the generous one, who was born not long after he reunited with his wife.

Crispin owned only one pair of pants and one shirt, he skipped meals frequently, and had no books of his own. He would borrow books from his classmates late at night when they were tired from studying, or early in the morning, an hour before exams. Despite extreme difficulties, he passed the bar examination with top honors, he obtained a perfect score in Mercantile Law because he was armed with exceptional brilliance and an excellent, and retentive, memory. Their second child, Cesar, the God-loving one, was born during Crispin's bar examination. Crispin juggled whatever free time he had between studies, work and assisting his wife at home.

The attack on Pearl Harbor was a surprise military strike by the Imperial Japanese Navy Air Service upon the United States naval base on Hawaii, the attack came on Sunday, December 7, 1941. At this time Crispin was an Intelligence Officer of JAGO (Judge Advocate General's Office) of the Armed Forces of the Philippines, tasked mainly in providing legal help to the military in all aspects as required. His undying love for his country inspired him to join the guerilla movement when he was about twenty-five years old. During the Japanese invasion of the Philippines, he fought alongside his countrymen and Americans.

He was away from home a lot and, by God's grace, Manuel, the only brother of Remedios, came to be with his family and assumed Crispin's responsibilities. Manuel was a priest who was granted a dispensation from the priesthood because of his severe asthma.

Manuel was a compassionate, God-fearing, selfless and patient man. He did everything in his power that was humanly possible to help Crispin's family. His love was the most valuable and appreciated gift he gave to the whole family. He was always available to lend an ear and a gracious helping hand with their day-to-day problems, hurts and pains. With empathy and compassion, he would counsel them and lead them in prayer, and would always be ready to assist with the children's schoolwork. More than a shoulder to cry on, he showed the importance of family and most of all, love, which was valued and instilled into the fragile minds of the children. He was so much loved by all.

During the Japanese invasion, Crispin was captured by the Japanese and taken to Fort Santiago to be beheaded. Later, he discovered it was a fellow Filipino who informed the Japanese officers that Crispin was an intelligence officer in the Philippine army. This Filipino was from the 'Makapili' group recruited by the Japanese. A Makapili is a patriotic association of Filipinos that was formed by the militants on December 8, 1944 during World War II which gave military aid to the Imperial Japanese Army. A massive manhunt for Crispin was launched until he was finally captured.

The prisoners at Fort Santiago were denied food and water and were confined to a dungeon. It was the Japanese goal to make them weak so they could not fight back and could not easily escape. During high tide, the water in the dungeon was up to their waists and they were left soaking in it, but they tried to drink from the muddy waters. Fort Santiago was close to the waters of Manila de Bay.

During the war the Japanese were cruel to their captives and subjected them to physical abuse and wanton killings. They starved their prisoners and those who could no longer go on were brutally beaten. They pulled out some of the prisoners' fingernails and others were burned with a cigarette butt. Some were bayoneted, shot and even beheaded on the spot by their captors.

At Fort Santiago, where Crispin was detained, the prisoners, who were reduced to skin and bones, were told to form a line when the beheading was scheduled. They began sobbing as they waited for this heinous incident to occur. Crispin instructed them not to cry and to show the Japanese that, *"We Filipinos know how to die for our country."* With great trust in the Almighty, Crispin was brave and ready to face his creator. He possessed an incredible strength and feared nothing because of his love for his country and undying faith in God.

While the prisoners were in line to be beheaded, Crispin did not expect a miracle was about to happen. One of the Japanese soldiers began calling out Crispin's name. He didn't respond right away because he was thinking, "I'm next." To find out who Crispin was, the Japanese soldier began lifting the prisoners' long and greasy hair away from their faces and checked them one by one. When one of the Japanese soldiers recognized Crispin, he took him aside and brought him to the Japanese officer. The officer loaded Crispin onto an enclosed truck which was used for food supplies. Crispin did not know why he was taken and loaded onto the truck. The truck was driven out of the huge garrison compound. To Crispin's surprise, he was set free and saved from being beheaded. Remedios's prayers had been answered!

Looking like a skeleton, weak, filthy and starved, he ran to the very first canal he saw and sipped the dirty water. The next thing he did was to wave down the first horse-drawn carriage he saw. When the coachman saw him, he raced away as fast as he could. The coachman thought he had seen a ghost.

Following Crispin's release, he ordered his men to bring to him every single Japanese soldier they captured, hoping he would find the one who had released him. He looked for him for several months, but to no avail. Later he learned that the Japanese soldier

had been killed. For the rest of his life, he prayed for him every
night.

EPISODE 2

THE MATRIARCH

Ever Patient One

"She opens her mouth with wisdom, and the teaching of kindness is on her tongue. She looks well to the ways of her household and does not eat the bread of idleness."- Proverbs 31-26-27.

Remedios, the mother of eight, was a walking image of class and grace. Feminine in her actions, she stood with impeccable posture and spoke in a gentle voice. One of her grandchildren described her this way: *"She did not put on airs of conceit and yet anyone who encountered her was captivated by her presence and the depths of her being. She had the stature of a queen, the appearance of a first lady, and always a demeanor filled with solemnity, dignity, and, above all, grace. Her heart was a vast ocean of love, patience, and understanding."*

Despite only having completed high school, she excelled in everything she did. There was no word she could not spell. She had excellent reading and writing skills and her math skill was outstanding. She got an excellent quality of education during those days.

Every morning, Remedios went to church before going to the market to buy fresh raw foods and ingredients for her family's delicious meals. Her constant focus was on preparing balanced meals that included meat or fish, vegetables and fruits. Food was one thing she would never skimp on. She wanted her family to be as healthy as they could be.

She was a full-time mom who never got tired. No matter what challenges she faced, or how exhausted she was, she continued to fulfill her duties and accepted her trials without complaints, sometimes drowning herself in tears and prayers. Despite heartaches, Remedios experienced countless moments of joy as well. She was a saint in Crispin's eyes and he loved her unconditionally. That was all that mattered to Remedios. Crispin often told his children, "You must always love your saintly mother."

Remedios found fulfillment as a wife and mother in being the best. Meticulously neat to a fault, she managed her household well and took good care of her children, even assisting them with their schoolwork. Kindness, perseverance, humility and love for one another were some lessons Remedios instilled in her children. As everyone went to bed at night, Remedios whispered, "Goodnight, sleep tight. Don't let the bugs bite, and don't forget to pray."

Remedios was frequently found kneeling in prayer in front of a large altar of religious statues which she decorated with roses from her garden. She loved roses and offered them to Jesus and the Blessed Mother with great joy. She prayed the rosary and novenas every day. Her favorite devotional songs were, Amazing Grace, How Great Thou Art, and Prayer of St. Francis. She frequently cited to her children, Matthew 23:12, which states, *"Those who exalt themselves will be humbled, and those who humble themselves will be exalted."*

The most important lesson Remedios taught her children was to trust and love God with all their hearts and souls. She raised her children by setting a good example in her own life, and by the power of her faith. What a true inheritance!

EPISODE 3

THE PATRIARCH

Principled, Patriotic and Brave

"Love bears all things, believes all things, hopes all things, endures all things." - 1 Corinthians 13:7

Crispin, aside from being a brilliant lawyer, was a caring person, selfless, forgiving and generous to a fault. He was a patriotic man of tenacity and courage who fought for what was right, regardless of the cost.

With strength and power in his voice, he commanded the attention of anyone. The energy in his voice was matched by an astounding eloquence and extensive vocabulary. With an unbelievable IQ, the strength of his convictions and beliefs earned great power and demanded respect.

Crispin also had an extremely sensitive side; he would give whatever he could to anyone in need. He had a big heart. It was his big heart that had been both a blessing and a misfortune when others took advantage of it.

Crispin was a strict disciplinarian and all his children feared him. Although he was strict, he was always fair. When they heard their father's bombastic voice echoing down the hall, everyone remained silent in their rooms. It was rare for him to get angry but, when he did, it was best not to provoke him.

Because he was worried about his children's safety, they only had friends who were chosen for them and they could only play in their own backyard. Being so protective, he wanted to have close supervision of all his children.

Learning from his past, having married before he got his degree, one of the most important rules he had for his children was that, if they married after they graduated from college, he didn't care who they married, or when they married. As is always the case in most families, one of his children would defy him.

Crispin faithfully attended to his duties as a husband and father. He worked hard, often both night and day, to provide for and raise his growing family, and was often seen in deep and solemn thoughts, overwhelmed by his fast-growing family and the responsibilities that came with it; but he never faltered and never lost hope with divine guidance.

Every day he could be found early in the morning meditating and praying in the garden, where only the soft whisper of the flowing water could be heard, the soft breeze could be felt and the graceful dancing of the leaves could be enjoyed. He marveled at nature's splendor and listened to its gentle breathing. He was always heard telling his children about the importance of the balance that exists on God's earth and everything in it. After his prayers, he would do his usual exercises and read. Reading was one of his obsessions and couldn't get enough of it.

The most essential lesson Crispin wanted to teach his kids was to have no fear of anything or anyone besides God and doing evil. "If you haven't done anything wrong to your fellow human beings, don't be afraid", he urged. He advised them to be grateful and to stop worrying about anything because God had made each of them enough. He revered our Lord the Almighty, who served as both his strength and his refuge.

Everyone has flaws, and Crispin was no exception. He was pledging his money to others, although he had not earned it. He became penniless because of his uncontrollable desire to always help and give. People took advantage of his generosity and his forgiving heart. This became a problem for Remedios.

His greatest weakness was women. He loved women, and women adored him. He was a dashing and handsome man with a lot of charm. His smile could light up a room and everyone wanted to be around him. His lustful pursuit of women became a source of problems in his family. His life seemed to have a pattern. He was involved in trying his best to eradicate graft and corruption. He earned vast wealth, lavished friends and helped others, went bankrupt, earned even more wealth and captivated woman after woman.

EPISODE 4

PERSEVERANCE

Will Endure

"Blessed is the one who perseveres under trial because, having stood the test, that person will receive the crown of life that the Lord has promised to those who love him."–James 1:12

In seeking to build their family, Remedios and Crispin prayed and asked God to show them how to strengthen the family's relationship with one another. They believed in prayers and were convinced that no matter what struggles may come along the way, nothing can replace the power of praying for their children. They had complete trust that when they call on the Lord, He will answer their prayers. God did more than they could ever have imagined. Seeing God answer their prayers and meet their needs strengthened their faith. *"Ask and you shall receive."* Luke 11:9-13.

Being Christian parents, they became students of the Lord, learning how to raise godly children. As role models they hoped that by praying fervently and showing genuine love for their children, they could improve family harmony and lay the groundwork for loving relationships that would last a lifetime.

To this day the Reyes family is closely knit. They remain God-fearing and God-loving people. Remedios and Crispin sacrificed a lot and worked tirelessly to raise their children to be productive members of society while keeping God at the center of their lives. They prayed and hoped for their children to love each other, trust each other, to support and always be there for one another. This was their dream, their obsession, and for them, the greatest gift they could give their children.

On January 12, 1943, they were blessed with a third child, Teresa, the resilient one. Teresa was born during the darkest period in Philippine history, the Japanese occupation, while Crispin, with unwavering spirit, fought in the war.

Remedios and Crispin persevered despite their hardships. Their situation became too difficult with Crispin's meager allowance, fighting in the war and raising three small children; but Remedios gave it her all and never stopped praying, always ready to accept whatever God had in store for them. She always said, *"El Hombre propone y Dios dispone."* (Man proposes, God disposes).

EPISODE 5

VICTORY

How Gracious Thou Art

"The righteous cry out, and the Lord hears them; He delivers them from all their troubles."- Psalm 34: 17-18.

On July 5, 1945, the US liberated the Philippines from the hands of the cruel Japanese, and the gruesome war finally ended. Some minor isolated guerrilla action in practically uninhabited mountain ranges occasionally persisted, but this great land mass of 120,000 square miles, with a population of a little over 100,000,000, was now freed of the invaders.

Victory came at a steep price, over 23,000 American military personnel and about 100,000 Filipinos were killed or captured during the 1941-1942 and 1944-1945 campaigns, this was a momentous occasion that saw MacArthur and his forces fulfill the promise made to their Filipino allies in the early dark days of the war, the famous - "I shall return". The Japanese formally signed the surrender on board the USS *Missouri* in Tokyo Bay on September 2, 1945, with the proceedings being overseen by General Douglas MacArthur.

Crispin was elated with joy at seeing the end of the war. He knew it meant the end of the destruction of communities and families; and of the disruption to the development of the social and economic fabric of his beloved nation.

Our Lord blessed them with their fourth child, the tireless Rosa, on June 3, 1945. What a wonderful welcome gift after the war, they thought.

Crispin was commended during the Liberation of the Philippines but refused to accept back pay because he said that his war services had no price tag. He served his country, not just willing to shed a tear, but truly ready to lay down his life, fortune and honor for the salvation of his country and its people, expecting nothing in return.

Crispin was blessed with unrivaled brilliance, resourcefulness, endurance and an unwavering desire to do much for his country, his fellow citizens and family, his crusade to serve never faltered. Now that the war was over and life became easier for his family, Crispin spent more time at home, but he remained busy as a lawyer.

Manuel, the only brother of Remedios, was a man of faith, God-loving, and kind, he stayed with the Reyes family and remained of service to all of them until he succumbed to asthma in 1957. Though Manuel was not healthy, always suffering from asthma and the challenges of life, he lived life the best he could and he never uttered a single word of complaint. He accepted his fate with humility. The family loved him and enjoyed spending time with him. The kids were always excited when he came home from work because he always brought them chocolates, popcorn, candies and other fun things that Manuel knew they would enjoy. He would dangle the treats in front of the kids, raising and lowering the goodies with a sweet smile, daring them to grab them from his grasp. This precious memory is forever ingrained in the children's minds, it is something that they would treasure for the rest of their lives.

Manuel enjoyed providing food for the pigeons that gathered on the roof of their neighbor's home. The pigeons had a schedule and would gather to eat from Manuel's kindness. One day Manuel experienced a severe asthma attack, he endured seventeen nonstop days of labored breathing and gasping for air. There was no asthma treatment on the market at that time. He had little appetite and seldom drank any water. The day before he passed away he requested ice cream; that he was now eating made everyone happy, they did not know that it was the last meal he would enjoy. He passed away the following day at around 6:00 p.m. The family then heard what they thought was children crying. They were shocked to discover that the noise was being made by a group of pigeons assembled on the roof. One pigeon flew inside the house and rested near Manuel's feet while he was lying in his casket. It crept all the way up beside his right shoulder, looking frail and dying, it then spread its wings before taking its last breath.

A few years passed. The family wanted their beloved uncle to be placed in Remedios's favorite church, so Manuel was exhumed. They were surprised to see the pigeon was still intact. There was not a single feather lost. They placed the pigeon with Manuel's remains in the church.

God blessed Remedios and Crispin with four more children. Consuelo, the astute one, was the fifth and the only child to be born skinny and sickly. Socorro, the sixth, was the shy and quiet one, Junior, the seventh, was the selfless one, and Jaime, the hardworking one, is the youngest.

EPISODE 6

PRECIOUS MOMENTS

Family Comes First

"The heart of man plans his way, but the Lord establishes his steps."–

Proverbs 16:9.

Many people think that leaving a legacy is solely about property and material wealth; they don't realize that the most significant legacies are acts of compassion and generosity, love for one's family and others, knowledge imparted, values inculcated and memories created.

Whether it's a charitable act, a vacation, a gathering, a story shared, or a celebration of special occasions such as births, weddings, Christmas or Thanksgiving, family traditions like these create indelible memories that will be ingrained in the children's minds for the rest of their lives. When shared with others, they also allow you to explain their importance to the next generation and beyond. They will forget their parents' house, cars and furniture; but they will never forget the legacy of love, kindness and charity. It is the greatest bequest one can leave behind.

Remedios and her family looked forward to Christmas every year. It was their favorite time… the birth of Jesus, a time for a grand celebration and togetherness. Her children were always dressed in fine clothing and they were fed the best and tastiest food money could buy. The children looked forward to the prosciutto from Italy that their mother always bought, the name translates to "ham" in Italian. It is made only from the hind legs of pigs and is aged during a dry-curing process. Remedios would run a ridiculously hot, large butcher's knife over the ham's surface, and everyone would enjoy and savor the aroma of the smoke produced by the sizzling sugar and fat of the ham's exterior. The children would be gathered around the table, excited, with their hands outstretched, unable to wait for their turn to get a piece. "Hmm, this is the most delicious ham, Mama." One child exclaimed.

As a tradition, the family went to midnight mass on Christmas Eve to commemorate the birth of our Lord Jesus Christ. That also meant feasting on *bibingka and puto bumbong*, chestnuts and other treats from vendors lined up in the churchyard while they were still hot off the grill. They walked to and from church, taking advantage of the beautiful weather with the smell of cold winter rain in the crisp air which was exhilarating.

Junior, the seventh child, was the artistic one and had imaginative decorating ideas about their home. They had a tree, Christmas lights and garlands. They made the Christmas tree out of white toilet paper, it looked like fresh snow and was stunning, adding a touch of elegance to their home. They had a handmade "parol," a lantern consisting of a five-sided star made of thin bamboo strips wrapped in multicolored crepe paper and cellophane, a light bulb hanging on the inside. The lantern was displayed in the window. Christmas was always a joyful and magnificent celebration representing a warm welcome for Jesus' birth.

One thing Remedios enjoyed doing was making flowers out of the straws that are usually used to make Hawaiian grass skirts. She spent hours hand-shaping multicolored straws into a variety of lovely flowers. The rainbow colors came to life in her arrangements. Remedios's favorite flowers were all kinds of roses, because of that, Consuelo continues to bring roses to her parents' final resting place to this day.

Remedios was a loving, kind and understanding mother. All her kids, especially Consuelo, felt very comfortable discussing anything with her and asking for her advice. One day, she confessed to her mother that she had a crush on this cute "mestizo" boy who attended the same school as her. Her mother made her happy by giving her sound advice, complete understanding and unwavering support. When Consuelo eventually told her she wanted to elope with her mestizo boy, her mother smiled and said nothing. She instead gave her PhP 6,000 pesos to spend.

You would catch them both shopping for fine jewelry during the weekends. Remedios did not buy any jewelry without the approval of Consuelo. Her taste in gold and diamonds was exquisite.

The eight siblings were blessed to have parents who loved them unconditionally. Their mother gave them exceptional care and was always available to help them with anything they needed. The eight children will always remember their mother as having a vast ocean of love and understanding in her heart.

Crispin, aside from being the best father and brother, was a philanthropist. He dedicated his life to his countrymen and took part in many charitable endeavors. He never stopped helping those in need, whether he knew them or not. Twenty-two of his nephews and nieces went to college and earned their degrees under his patronage. He always provided them, and all his siblings, with everything they needed, without them even asking.

He was a distinguished lawyer who held challenging and prestigious positions throughout his life. On May 5, 1965, he was the speaker of the Philippine Veterans at the World Veterans Federation Conference in Lausanne, Switzerland. He gave a rousing speech against the raging USA-Russia Cold War and the need to save all humanity from nuclear bombs, his desire was to unite all the people on our planet Earth. Crispin spoke of his dream of seeing nations living together in peace. His eloquent presentation moved the delegates and officials to such an extent that they gave him a standing ovation before forming a receiving line so that they could shake the hand of this great man. His profound ideas gave him great influence and respect.

The speech he gave was eloquent. "There should be no Cold War. We need to preserve the world. Nuclear weapons must not be used to destroy it. Almighty God gave us this world as our home and to provide for our needs."

No matter how busy Crispin was, he always had time for everything. On the weekends he took care of his plants and animals. In his yard he had chickens, rabbits, a monkey and a dog. He had fruit-bearing trees and he was overjoyed when they bore fruit. God's creations and everything in nature fascinated him.

He took great pleasure in making his wife and children happy and giving them an enjoyable life. On the weekends he looked forward to taking his children to the beach, horseback riding or picnics by the ocean and rivers. As they prepared to leave, Crispin would tell his children to hurry and attempt to leave their mother behind, because their mother knew he was teasing her, she didn't get upset and just smiled. He wanted to take them to as many places as he could, including the first mall ever constructed. They went to each new restaurant that opened, to the farmers' ranch, the carnival around Christmas, and many other places.

One day their father took them on a picnic by a beautiful river. Crispin saw a parade of large black ants. He wondered how the ants tasted. "It's bitter and spicy," he said after eating one. He was curious to know where they came from so he followed the trail, he was shocked to discover it came from a pile of feces, he puked on the spot and learned never to eat ants again.

These are the kinds of memories children will cherish forever. If the children had a good time, even if they don't remember it, that's nothing to sneeze at when developing a positive outlook on life. Precious and loving memories create an expectation that the world is a pleasant place. The Reyes children have many priceless memories that will stay with them for the rest of their lives, and are worthy of sharing with the world.

EPISODE 7

LITMUS TESTS OF FAITH

One for Ripley's

"Blessed are those who have not seen and yet have believed."–
John 20:29

Men have conquered the moon, but not the deep blue sea. Scientologists and atheists dispel faith by relying solely on themselves as if they have a crystal ball and the power to create a blade of grass. None of us have lived long enough to understand why countless "elements" or "mystical creatures" exist on mother Earth; why they exist, why God allows them to exist, and why we live among them. No human being, regardless of faith or religion, can comprehend their existence.

During the mid-1960s, Crispin purchased their first lot in Retiro, Quezon City, and built their own home. This was a neighborhood with thriving commercial stores, it is one of Metro Manila's largest. It didn't take long for unexplained events to occur, especially at night. These "mystical elements" were encountered by the family.

The room in one corner of the second floor of the house was occupied by the seventh and eighth children, Junior and Jaime. All the other six children were in the other rooms, also on the second floor. A massive pine tree stood at the corner of the house where the bedroom of Junior and Jaime was located. Almost instinctively, at the stroke of midnight, Junior opened his eyes and looked straight out of the window. What he witnessed was beyond anyone's comprehension. There was a tall, strange-looking creature standing there. It's known as "kapre" in the Philippines. It's not just any kapre, but one with a golden crown who is staring back at Junior, smiling and smoking a massive cigar. He was playful, swaying his head to the left and right. This happened three nights in a row. Then a huge black boar appeared, floating by the windowsill at around the same time. Unconvinced by what he saw, Junior blinked his eyes several times but the creature stayed there. He couldn't believe what he saw.

Kapre, the name of which is taken from the Arabic word *kafir* meaning "non-believer", can stand up to 9 foot tall, and is a hairy and muscular creature. People believe that this creature, or element, can transform into various animals. Kapres are said to live in massive old trees such as acacias, mangoes, bamboo and banyan (known in the Philippines as balete).

Although the kapre was playful to Junior, it picked on Jaime for some unknown reason. Jaime experienced intermittently elevated body temperatures. No doctor could explain the cause of the high fever. When Crispin, fearlessly and overconfidently, tried to gain control of the situation by intimidating, cursing and inviting the kapre to a duel, Jaime became sicker, eventually suffering with delirium.

Crispin came home one day with two "albulario" recommended by a friend, because Jaime was getting worse. The term "albulario" is derived from the Spanish word *herbolario*, which means "herbalist". They are sometimes referred to as witch doctors who can summon the spirits of the dead and other unknown elements. They could cast these elements out of the possessed person. It worked somehow! Jaime got better.

In the same location, Junior also saw a "tikbalang", a tall, long-limbed and bony human-like creature having the head and hooves of a horse. When sitting, its knees reached above its head. It just sat there and stared at him. Junior thought he was hallucinating. He again blinked his eyes several times because he could not believe what he saw--still it was there!

In other different places, he had seen playful dwarfs like those we see in the Snow White movie, he also saw Cupid, a little winged child with a bow and arrow like those in Valentine's cards, and the Holy Spirit as a blinding white dove descending upon his daughter's head while she was being christened. Nothing in this world could ever describe its celestial and heavenly beauty. Nothing in this world could explain to Junior all those things he saw that are out of this world!

They later discovered that the lot where their home was built was once a Japanese garrison in which people were tortured and killed, and that it had been converted into a cemetery during WWII.

Retiro was a place for festivities and celebrations. It was a place where suitors came, a child got married and angels were born, it was also a point of immigration to America, everyone there knew your name. One can only imagine how Remedios and Crispin managed all the obligations and responsibilities of such a large and growing family, let alone those unexplained, and seemingly never-ending, encounters.

It was in 1966 when their first child, Cecilia, left for the USA. She wanted to pursue a career in medical technology after successfully getting a bachelor's degree in Pharmacy and passing the board. Cecilia was, and is, a thoughtful, caring and generous person. She has a kind heart and is always willing to help. She is religious and a devout Catholic.

God's presence in her life was not only felt, but also seen. When she was young, she saw a vision of the Holy Family standing in front of their door while she was playing in the early evening. A bright light encircled them and remained for a minute. Mother De la Rosa (Mother of Sorrows) was also seen by Cecilia and her siblings, Teresa, Cesar and Rosa, at around 2:00 p.m. reflected on the wall. It stayed there for a couple of minutes. Their father went through something similar. He saw Jesus when he joined the Cursillo in the late 1960s. Cursillo is a short informal spiritual retreat held by a group of Roman Catholics, organized mainly by lay people and originally established in Spain in 1944. Indeed, the family had some unbelievable life experiences.

Successful in completing her medical technology degree, Cecilia started working at Christ Hospital in Jersey City as a phlebotomist and remained there for almost four years. She got married to a navy corpsman in 1970.

In that same year, their fourth child, Rosa, eloped with her boyfriend, a classmate in medicine. As always, their parents were very supportive of them. Rosa had already graduated from college when she decided she wanted to marry. They got married on July 29, 1970. They had their firstborn in 1971 whom they would leave behind with Remedios because Rosa and her husband had to migrate to the US as medical exchange students. Remedios and Socorro brought the child to the USA to join them the following year.

Rosa was an untiring, persistent and stubborn child. She had a very determined personality, she worked hard to accomplish her goals. She kept nagging you until she got what she wanted, and if she did not, she would throw a tantrum, pull out her hair, stomp her feet and cry like a spoiled brat. When she did not like the way her mother fixed her hair, she would adopt that bratty behavior.

Despite this, her mother would re-do her hair lovingly, and with a smile.

Despite her forceful personality and stubborn nature, Rosa often had trouble making decisions on her own. She would always ask her siblings what to do, even on trivial matters. The only certainties in her life seemed to be her career and her choice of a spouse, which was a big blessing for her. She married a man who had an abundance of patience for her stubbornness, hot-headedness and domineering personality.

Rosa got first pick of her father's gifts whenever he came home from trips abroad because if she was not given that privilege, she would throw a tantrum and she would complain. She was the princess/senorita of the family.

One unforgettable event for Rosa happened during her childhood days. She wanted to accompany her parents whenever they went out. She always wanted to go, although she often got sick and throwing up in the car.

One day, Crispin wanted to take their mother on a date. Rosa insisted on going with them and no explanations could persuade her to stay at home. Crispin found out how persistent and annoying she could be. Crispin could not win against Rosa, so he relented and took her with them, but that was after he spanked her. She cried so hard all the way to the car until she was at the point of throwing up when a police officer stopped them. Her father told the officer he was taking his child to the hospital, the officer did not give Crispin a ticket. Rosa's stubbornness paid off on that occasion.

Her mother would always call Rosa during her medical internship to ask what she wanted to eat. Remedios made sure that someone took her food to the hospital where she was interning. Junior would always be the one to bring her hot, delicious food. Rosa knew and felt that her mother loved her so much.

Though everyone was busy with many things going on in their lives, the family continued to experience unexplained encounters with the underworld. The concept of an underworld is found not just in the Reyes family, but also in almost every civilization and such encounters may be as old as humanity itself. According to myths and religious beliefs, the underworld is the place where the souls of the dead go, and it has always been believed that this destination is under the earth or below the world of the living. It is, however, important to note that the underworld in many cultures is not entirely evil, but just a destination where the dead go to receive judgment for their lives on Earth. Some call them earthbound.

The Reyes family had their accounts of encounters, both with the eerie and the divine. They had a collection of extraordinary, miraculous experiences and hair-raising and terrifying tales. Such bizarre events are so strange and unbelievable, but they were experienced, heard, felt, and seen… some of them for "Ripley's Believe it or Not!"

EPISODE 8

LOVE OF GOD, COUNTRY AND MAN

Truth and Justice Prevail

"Blessed is a man who perseveres under trial; for once he has been approved, he will receive the crown of life which the Lord has promised to those who love Him."–James 1:2.

Crispin saw an opportunity to help advance the Philippine legislation during the 1970 Constitutional Convention which was tasked with reviewing and updating the 1935 Constitution. His intention was to assist in drafting the new constitution from the old constitution, contributing his experiences, ideas and beliefs in order to better the country. Unfortunately, his noble intention did not materialize because he lost in the election for representatives to the constitutional convention.

One of President Marcos' legal advisors was Crispin. When he witnessed the president's egregious corruption, he advised him to stop countless times. He resigned as the president's legal counsel after the president ignored his advice. He had no intention of being a part of the president's insatiable corruption.

Crispin's unwavering patriotism compelled him to combat corruption in the Philippine government. He valiantly faced all the public and private sector's biggest scoundrels, thieves and robbers.

He would sacrifice everything for his nation. The following is an excerpt from his speech to the Filipino people:

Let us not despair with more abuses and sufferings,

the more, the better, then greater vigilance will rise.

Get over with the worst, for afterward comes hope.

Darkness will soon unfold the breaking of a beautiful dawn.

While Crispin was preoccupied with his endeavours, Consuelo eloped and married the son of a Spanish professor in 1968. She was the only child who defied her father's rule that one must finish college before marrying. Consuelo and her husband were only nineteen, but Crispin and Remedios were incredibly supportive, giving them one of the most lavish weddings they could have imagined and hired a famous couturiere for Consuelo's bridal gown. Her mother bought the most stunning diamond wedding rings. Consuelo, who was still young and carefree, did nothing to prepare for the wedding and simply showed up. Their wedding photos were plastered across three major Manila newspapers the day after the wedding.

Although Consuelo married before completing her degree and was frequently ill, she finished college. Her father did not know that despite Consuelo always being sick, she was taking night classes. He thought she would never graduate from college. When

Consuelo presented her diploma to her parents they were happy and welled with pride and joy.

"Do not be afraid of anyone except God, " Crispin told his children. He added, "Never be ashamed if you have done nothing wrong to your fellowmen." Crispin's words were etched in his children's minds. Consuelo may be sickly and weak, but she was not afraid of anything; this is most likely why she was not afraid to defy her own father's rule about marriage. Occasionally her father referred to her as a lioness.

One year after Consuelo got married, Crispin established the Anti-Graft League of the Philippines (AGLP) in 1969 and it became the primary focus of his life's work. The Anti-Graft League of the Philippines was founded as a non-governmental, non-stock and nonprofit organization. The aim of the AGLP was to protect the interests of the Republic, its instrumentalities and political subdivisions, as well as its constituents, from abuses committed by its public officials and employees, elected or otherwise. Crispin's love and commitment to the Filipino people would not allow him to abandon his crusade, despite Crispin's description of it as a *"hopeless war against corruption."*

His heart was filled with love for his homeland and he was determined to continue fighting for the oppressed. He would shed blood and die to save his countrymen from the shame, crime and injustice that had befallen them. For accusing and prosecuting major corrupt government officials, he was incarcerated for almost two years during martial law.

"The fight against this cancerous disease of graft and corruption must be a national effort... a total, unrelenting movement under the nation's leader who must be resolutely and honestly dedicated to our country and people. Indeed, history has shown that a national crusade, a sweeping social movement, and a moral revolution are sparked from above by a mature and respected good leader who has captured the imagination of a suffering people and united them for moral rebirth and greatness. If we fail, it is undoubtedly a failure of leadership. Where is then the man to lead us? Come, your unhappy people, clamor to touch the hem of your garment." (The Nation Magazine, 1970, Anti-Graft League of the Philippines)

"Do we have to undergo the supreme test of the very bloody American Civil War, French, and other revolutions to temper in the fiery crucible our democratic maturity and for moral deliverance and rebirth of our people from so much corruption, shame, and crime? Where are those truly brave hearts among Filipinos, the courageous citizens of the nation, who not just shed a tear, but are truly prepared to lay down their life, fortune and honor for the salvation of our country and the people?"–Crispin T. Reyes (CTR).

His crusade against graft and corruption spanned forty-five long, miserable, agonizing years of service to his country, always striving to protect the public interest and always keeping the oath, *"Do no harm"*. He gave his life to his country, not for fame, fortune or glory, but because it was the right thing to do. He suffered unjust persecution for the sake of his people.

In 1970, their second child, Cesar, migrated to the United States; he got married shortly after arriving. He was, and remains, a gentle, humble and thoughtful man who always gives the benefit of the doubt to others. Sometimes his unending benefit of the doubt goes beyond logic. He is unaffected by his surroundings because he believes everything happens for a reason. Jesus is his greatest love, in whom he has complete faith and trust and to whom he has always surrendered everything.

Acting frequently as if he is the oldest, he does his best to assist and advise whenever there is a problem in the family. His conscience tells him he must do the right thing. Honesty and fairness make him a true peacemaker.

One of his most treasured memories was when he was a little child and got sick. He was lying on his back with a high fever, his head on his mother's lap while his mother caressed his forehead and prayed for her son's healing. Miraculously his fever was gone by the end of the day. Cesar's faith in God was strengthened and he witnessed, and felt, his mother's tender love for him.

On September 21, 1972, President Marcos declared martial law. Crispin was on the list of people who would be detained according to an intelligence report. He could move around freely for a little over a month after martial law was declared. He became complacent so he went back to his AGLP office in Ermita, Manila. One day the military soldiers raided the AGLP office; Crispin was arrested and all his documents were confiscated. Being astute he quickly disposed of his black book which contained all the names of his supporters and other contacts, he wanted to protect them. This book was never found by the authorities. As a former intelligence officer, he was aware of the standard military procedures, thus he was left with no option but to follow willingly and silently.

He was first brought to Camp Crame for interrogation, he remained there for several weeks. Camp Crame is the Philippine National Police headquarters. Later he was transferred to Fort Bonifacio in Taguig, Metro Manila. When President Marcos declared martial law in the Philippines in 1972, Fort Bonifacio became the site of three detention centers housing political prisoners. Some of the country's leading academics, creative writers, journalists, historians and other major political figures were among the prisoners Crispin joined. Food and water were rationed to the inmates.

Remedios and Socorro were in the US when Crispin was arrested. Upon hearing of the sad news, Remedios got so worried and wanted to go home immediately, and so they hurriedly booked a flight back to the Philippines.

1973 came and went, and 1974 arrived. Knowing about Crispin's incarceration, his friends and supporters lobbied military generals, including the Minister of Defense, for his release, but it was all for naught. They claimed that Crispin's incarceration was ordered by President Marcos himself. President Marcos must still be bitter from when Crispin resigned as his legal counsel. The president knew Crispin could topple his regime and so he had to be silenced.

Crispin was imprisoned for over twenty months and lost approximately twenty pounds in weight, during this time he grew a foot-long beard. Despite the lack of food and water, he remained sharp and focused. He never lost his fighting spirit. God was his source of strength and refuge. One day he learned he would be transferred to some unknown place in the middle of the darkest night. Crispin knew it meant he would be killed, so he took action. Crispin instructed Consuelo's husband to report this plan to the camp commander, Brigadier General Fidel Ramos. Fortunately, he was not moved from where he was detained, obviously it was not his time yet. God always watches. With no charge brought against Crispin, he was finally released in June 1974.

The Marcos regime, which ruled the impoverished Philippines with an iron fist, was plagued with unbelievable levels of corruption. The World Bank and UN Office on Drugs and Crimes said Marcos, having the longest reign as dictator, stole between $5 billion and $10 billion from the country's coffers. The dictatorship was deadly, especially for those who stood against Marcos, they were killed or simply 'went missing'. Crispin was one of the lucky ones who escaped this atrocious crime by the Marcos regime.

Crispin, despite being wrongfully imprisoned without being charged for two long years, had no animosity toward Marcos. The agony of the Filipino people under the Marcos government would soon be over. Nothing in this world is everlasting. Everything has an end. The twenty-year dictatorship of President Ferdinand Marcos, a lawyer, dictator and kleptocrat, came to an end in 1986.

On May 14, 1972, their third child, Teresa, married a lawyer who was her classmate. She is an honest, upright, and well-meaning person. When Teresa was a young child, their mother relied on Teresa to do the shopping and cooking while her mother was in the hospital because of a recurring hemorrhage. Remedios showed Teresa how to cut a string bean when preparing for cooking. Teresa precisely cut the string beans according to the example. In her young mind, each piece had to be cut exactly like the sample or it would not cook. Because Teresa did such an excellent job that Remedios relied on her to do more housework.

Her mother believed she could outperform everyone because she was the brightest. She gradually gained more responsibilities, such as cleaning the house, washing the dishes and running errands here and there. Sometimes Remedios forgot that Teresa, despite her youth, was exhausted. Teresa did everything her mother asked of her without complaint.

Teresa wondered, "Why should it always have to be me? Do they not care enough about me?" For years those questions went unanswered. Teresa was convinced that her mother did not love her.

Teresa did her best to show them her love and concern, hoping and believing that one day they would love her more. Teresa decided to never complain, demand anything, or be a burden to them. She believed she was loved less than the others. That belief persisted until it became ingrained in her personality. Because of these thoughts she became distracted and could not really focus. Her father noticed the change but never inquired why. Teresa's father advised her not to drive, but she was determined to succeed. Her ability to concentrate took years to develop, but she was successful.

EPISODE 9

TURNING POINT

Open My Eyes Lord

"He brought them out of darkness and the shadow of death and broke their chains in pieces."- Psalms 107:14.

The discovery of oneself - one's "true" self - is perhaps the most important defining moment in anyone's life. It is referred to as the "turning point." Finding yourself may appear to be a selfish goal, but it is a selfless process that is at the heart of everything we do in life.

Who am I? To be a valuable person on the planet, to be the best partner, parent, brother, sister and so on, we must first understand and know ourselves. What do we value and what can we offer? We need to remove layers of our lives that no longer serve us or reflect our true selves. It is resurrecting all our best selves that have been lost along the way, developing self-confidence, recognizing who we want to be and embarking on our unique destiny, whatever that may be. It is about recognizing and understanding our personal power while remaining open to our experiences.

After Crispin's release from prison, their sixth child, the quiet Socorro, married in September 1974. Socorro and her husband lived with her in-laws for the first two years of their marriage, it was a temporary arrangement until they moved to a small apartment. Socorro is fair and people sometimes refer to her as snow-white. She is shy, quiet and has a soft-spoken manner, but behind that facade is a forceful and feisty personality. She is determined and will go to any lengths to achieve her goal, no matter what the cost.

As an authoritative mother and wife, she runs a matriarchal household. Her timid husband and three sons fear her and, even as adults, still listen to their mother and do everything she tells them.

One of Socorro's fondest recollections was when she was a young child and yearned to play outside of their home but could not do so. She tried but could not succeed because she did not know how to go down the stairs, there was a small fence blocking them. Socorro, being persistent and determined, asked for Consuelo's help. Her older sister taught her to place a chair next to the fence so she could climb over it. Socorro was overjoyed when she finally overcame the fence blocking her way. She and Consuelo have been best friends for many years. They were like peas in a pod. They were classmates from first grade until the second year of college when they had to be separated because they took different majors.

In the same year that Socorro got married, Crispin joined the "De Colores" Ministry of the "Cursillo" Movement. This was shortly after Crispin's release from martial law incarceration. "De Colores" refers to Christ's many colors and "Cursillo" refers to a short course in Christianity - a Roman Catholic Church apostolic movement, founded on love, not law. In the Cursillo movement, being "in colors" means being "in God's grace." The Cursillo, an international organization, first established in Spain in 1944, was brought to the Philippines by the United States in 1963, and was then taken to the rest of Asia.

After the Cursillo, Crispin had a spiritual awakening which gave him an indescribable sense of deep inner knowing and understanding of his true nature. He had truly been spiritually reborn! High in spirit, he gave his children a handwritten letter as his gift to them, and it said:

To my children:

Let this brief testimonial serve as my lasting gift for all seasons. You know my very humble birth. I had to overcome tremendous hardships to finish my studies and to support you all. Despite the vagaries of my karmic fate, we got a little somewhere with the faith and devotion of your most wonderful, loving mother.

I have left intermittently the warmth of home leading a shameless, wayward life. You, my angelic children, and your saintly mother suffered much as a consequence. Even now, I know you suffer from deep anguish because I continue to hurt your feelings with my vicious diversion.

I do know that instead of your angry recriminations, you still give me your affection, and what is more, all of you still continue to help me with your prayers that I may rise and never fall again. You have really given me charity, not taunts, and abiding love, not hate, in your charitable hearts.

You must truly know, though I suffer painful remorse of conscience and I must say I am quite ashamed to all of you, especially to our Almighty Creator for all my grievous sins and grave shortcomings. Please forgive me.

Now I solemnly vow to you and our Lord God that there will be an absolute end to all this. Truly, I have already started to be a new man, a man of God. I really mean what I say in my concluding plea for the gospel. This is now my holy obsession.

Your continued sincere prayer will give me more strength and help me much to be spiritually REBORN again. And I implore the Holy Spirit to give you sustaining divine light, and may our loving Lord God give you His eternal blessings always.

Love to dearest Nanay, and to you all, my beloved children.

Love,

Tatay (father) 12/31/78

Crispin, as a speaker for the Cursillo movement, also gave his speech/prayer to the "cursillistas" at the end of the retreat:

Concluding Plea

"Let us resolve this Christmas season, for all seasons, this coming new year, not later when the darkening twilight of our life has overtaken us, but now, and forever, to dedicate ourselves to our Lord God and Almighty Creator of all universe, all things, including the proud mortal man who is just an atomic spiritual speck in all creation. Hence, let us love sincerely our Lord God above all with all our mind, heart, and soul, the first and highest commandment, and let us truly love one another, which is the second highest divine injunction. Let us do so always with charitable thoughts, words, acts, deeds, and conduct in our daily life towards our fellowmen regardless of social station, race, color, politics, sect, or religion. Let us now resolve against social hypocrisy, racial prejudice, religious intolerance, and bigotry, and espouse actively ecumenism for the salvation of all mankind."

"Let us also reform first ourselves and cultivate true humility and charity, which are the foundation of all virtues. Let us practice daily meditation to be nearer to our Lord God, commune always with our merciful Creator, and seek first His kingdom within us,

not beyond the clouds, moon, or stars, but in our heart and soul, within our blessed, though miserable human body which is the temple of the living God. And when we shall have done all this, despite our repeated spiritual rise and fall in the past, if we continue to rise thereafter, never to fall permanently again, and finally, if we are completely REBORN spiritually, then our holy dream and yearning to be accepted in our Father's house, where there are many mansions, will ultimately be crowned with blissful UNION with our merciful, loving God in all His glory in the highest celestial home where we shall find eternal harmony and peace and happily return to paradise."

EPISODE 10

THE JOURNEY

Time Traveled

"Seek the Kingdom of God above all else, and live righteously, and he will give you everything you need." -Matthew 6:33

Members of the Reyes family continued to have out-of-this-world experiences. Unseen forces followed them wherever they went. Consuelo, the fifth child, thought ghosts were only for the insane until she and her family encountered them. They can still feel, hear and see these unseen spirits today.

In the early part of 1975, the family moved to Santo Domingo, Quezon City, to a place larger than their Retiro home. Several cousins from the province stayed with them so that they could be close to their universities. Unseen spirits haunted the family once more, although the siblings appeared to be getting used to it.

Grown siblings and cousins shared many pleasant memories in this house. Despite their good fortune, the Reyes' faced foreclosure on their home. Crispin's proclivity for giving away his money did not help their situation. As a result, the siblings pooled their funds and saved the property.

It was that same year, 1975, when their youngest, Jaime, the hard-working one, migrated to the US to try a new life. He was not quite happy with the degree he got, so he took computer classes at New York University and graduated with a degree in computer science.

Jaime, being the youngest, got most of their parents' attention, as is often the case when you're the baby of the family. He was undoubtedly the favorite child.

He will say nothing negative about anyone because he has a kind heart. "There are always two sides to every coin," he frequently said. He always gives the benefit of the doubt until someone goes against the people he cares about the most.

He is thoughtful and humble. With endless patience and diligence, he gets things done immaculately. He personally renovated almost his entire house and he did an excellent and professional job!

During their childhood days, Jaime and Junior were best friends, having an age difference of two years. They shared a bedroom, went to school together and climbed giant trees together. They enjoyed climbing trees and staying there while eating the fruits they found. After eating the fruits they planted the seeds in empty milk cans. On special occasions they went shopping together to find gifts for their mother. They enjoyed each other's company immensely. Through college they partied on weekends until the wee hours of the morning.

Jaime was only eight years old when he began campaigning for his father who was running for the position of congressional representative in Bataan. He saw his father give speech after speech in various places, this inspired him. During one campaign, he wore a shirt with a photo of his father and the words written on it, "Reyes for Congressman". He boarded a jeepney with other passengers and campaigners and began yelling, "Parents, brothers, sisters, vote Reyes for Congressman!"

In 1978, the Reyes family moved to Matapat, Quezon City. This will become known as the ancestral home. The house was larger than the one in Santo Domingo. It has beautiful marble floors and elegant wide staircases made of narra wood. A narra wood is a large deciduous reddish hardwood tree native to most Asian countries. It is usually red or rose in color, and it is frequently variegated with yellow. It is one of the most expensive woods in the Philippines and it makes elegant staircases. It is the national tree of the Philippines.

The house is white, has five large bedrooms and a spacious, elegant marble balcony fronting the second floor. The balcony stretches across the entire front of the house, with exquisite, large columns. This was where Crispin did his routine morning exercises. Their home was quite large and had some amazing features. In terms of unseen spirits however, this house proved to be no different from the previous ones. They were haunted yet again.

They gradually accumulated opulent furnishings, appliances and draperies. Socorro soon moved in with them from her small apartment. She would stay with her parents for many years, caring for them and offering help whenever it was needed. She enjoyed staying with her parents and chose not to pursue a career in her field. She loved being a full-time stay-at-home mother and wife.

Socorro was frequently seen praying and going to church, whenever she heard that someone needed prayers, she would be there praying for them. She immersed herself in prayers, rosaries and novenas and went to church as often as she could. To this day you can always hear her talking about God and how much she trusts and believes in Him whenever she converses with someone.

In April 1981, Consuelo and her family, who were also living with her parents, had to migrate to the United States soon after Socorro moved in. Their father wanted them all to leave the Philippines for political and economic reasons.

The Reyes family had many blessings, but they also had many challenges. Despite Crispin's vagrancies and wayward behavior, Remedios kept the family together; she was the source of light and strength in their home and God gave her the graces she needed. Crispin admired and adored Remedios even more because of her unfailing love, understanding and devotion.

Insurmountable challenges remained, but Remedios and Crispin bravely faced them together, always united, their children remained obedient, supportive and loving to one another. Their unwavering commitment not only enabled their children to earn degrees in their respective fields of study, but also ensured that they remained steadfast in their love and support for each other. They raised eight godly children who grew up to be good people and valuable members of society. What an incredible accomplishment!

EPISODE 11

FAMILY CORPORATION

Foresight

"The heart of man plans his way, but the Lord establishes his steps."–Proverbs 16:9

Crispin started acquiring properties as he reached the height of his career. When he required money he would mortgage those very same properties. He needed money to fund all the cases and transactions that he did for his country in addition to the various expenses he had for the family. He was willing to spend everything he had for his beloved country. While some properties were never saved, others were. Could acquiring these properties be the beginning of something positive?

In 1979 Crispin founded their family corporation and called Alliance Management Corporation (AMC). He wanted the corporation to have control over all family assets, including their ancestral home, Matapat. He appointed the board's five members, excluding himself. Consuelo's husband, Fred, was appointed president, Teresa as treasurer, her husband Jun as secretary, Junior as a board member and Socorro's husband as vice president. Junior succeeded Fred who migrated to the United States with his family in 1981, they also added Socorro as an additional board member.

As they gained more properties, they were all titled under AMC and placed under its management, except for two properties, one of which they called the Subdivision and the other they called the Bridge which was placed under the name of Junior. Crispin's directive was for Teresa, being the family's lawyer, to hold all property titles. However, Teresa never took possession of any titles because they could not be found.

Crispin had a soft spot for the Bataan properties among all other properties. Originally, it was a one-piece real estate property comprising over 16-hectares. During the Marcos regime a highway was constructed, dividing the property into two. Thereafter, Crispin had these two properties and other adjacent properties further subdivided which they referred to as a Subdivision and a Farmhouse. The former is three hectares in size comprising six-lots, while the latter is two and a half hectares and comprising five-lots. Since the area is fast developing into commercial usage, these properties are currently worth hundreds of millions of Philippine pesos if offered on the market.

With Crispin's foresight he saw the need for the establishment of the family corporation, especially since he had so many children. He wished to safeguard all properties, and most important of all, avoid any unnecessary future issues that most families face.

EPISODE 12

PATIENCE AND DETERMINATION

Never Give Up

"I will instruct you and teach you in the way you should go; I will counsel you with my loving eye on you."–Psalm 32:8.

A man of integrity, Junior, the seventh child, has endless patience and understanding. He is selfless, always gives the benefit of the doubt and is prepared to forgive and forget. He devotes his life to helping others. Family is of utmost importance to him and he would do anything for them.

From the simple cleaning of whatever needed to be cleaned, going to the wet market and neighborhood stores several times a day, feeding and attending to the chickens from incubation to the harvesting of eggs... Junior, as a young child, already had responsibilities placed on his young forming shoulders. Besides these responsibilities he also had to look after their father's animals. Because the family couldn't have a water supply on the second floor where they were all living, Junior was tasked with bringing buckets of water from the deep well reservoir on the first floor and carrying them up the steep stairs to the second floor. The bucket of water he had to carry daily was almost as heavy as him.

On Sundays, in the late afternoons, he walked alone to church. Even though the mass was in Latin, he would attend because it was the only time he could after he had finished his chores. Sometimes the entire family went out to dinner while he was designated as the house guardian.

His mother told him he needed to be considerate to all his siblings, which made him wonder, *"why me? I am the second youngest."* When he was a child and felt lonely, he would tell himself, *"I am also a creation of God. I'll leave it to the Lord. I know this won't last forever, but there will always be a tomorrow."*

Despite his struggles, trials and tribulations, he did not harbor an iota of resentment or bitterness in his heart. The invisible healed scars, varying in width, length and depth, remained within his persona. The shadows of those years would stay with him.

Junior moved to the United States in 1983 with his wife, who was expecting their first child, to try a new life. He had difficulty finding work since no one wanted to hire him because he was overqualified and lacked local experience. The young family made do with whatever they could find in dumpsters, such as a vacuum cleaner and other useful items. They used boxes for tables and had a single-layer mattress on the floor. They lived in a tiny apartment.

He and his wife accepted whatever jobs were available. They would jump for joy whenever they received a good tip. He worked tirelessly to advance in the food industry and, without disclosing his true education and professional experience, he rose to the position of manager--eventually he was able to open his own restaurant.

People underestimate the difficulty of succeeding in the restaurant industry. People who are successful in other businesses believe they will be successful restaurateurs. Junior was successful in his profession in the Philippines, but will he be as successful in the restaurant business? Filled with hope and ambition, they set out on their restaurant adventure.

They had the best Mexican restaurant in Sun City, Arizona. People would travel miles to experience Junior's best-tasting foods. Some of these people from the east, who traveled hundreds of miles, are called snowbirds. Unfortunately Junior couldn't afford to hire all the help they needed to run the restaurant because they didn't have enough capital. He and his wife ran the restaurant with a little help from his two young children and one hired help. The restaurant survived for two years. The daily grind of opening the restaurant before the sun rises, and closing late at night, wore him down to the point where they had to sell the business--but only after they had purchased a beautiful home and a family car. Junior's hard work and dedication enabled them to live a comfortable life.

Meanwhile, while everyone in the family was living their carefree lives, the AMC went dormant and nearly became extinct.

They also neglected their properties in Bataan, which became inhabited by squatters. Taxes that were overdue were not paid and were completely forgotten. Part of the property became the city's open garbage dump.

In June 1988, Teresa received a letter from her mother that touched her heart. In the letter Remedios was bequeathing her most prized diamond ring to Teresa. This ring had been given as a gift by Crispin to Remedios. She also wanted Teresa to have her pair of diamond earrings, another ring and a big diamond cross, in addition to the money in her bank account. Teresa thought to herself, *"Oh my God, she loved me after all."* She closed her eyes after reading her mother's letter and said in a whisper, *"Thank you, Lord, for answering my prayers. You gave me the love of my mother that I had yearned for. Above and beyond those material things, my mother's love was the most important thing to me."*

When Teresa was in the USA, she opened a bank account in her own name and included her mother's name; her mother also deposited funds into this account. When Teresa returned to the Philippines she did not close the account, Teresa regularly received the bank statements from Remedios, she had more than $10,000 in it, this was the money mentioned in her mother's letter.

Teresa's belief that her mother did not love her instantly vanished! God reveals things in His own unique way.

EPISODE 13

PERSEVERANCE

Always Be Considerate To Others

"Let us not become weary in doing good, for at the proper time, we will reap a harvest if we do not give up."–Galatians 6:9

In April 1998, Junior and his family returned to the Philippines to celebrate his wife's parents wedding anniversary. They were getting old and wanted to share this special occasion with them. He told his wife that if they returned home, they would not go back to the United States because starting over would be extremely difficult. They never did return, except to visit their children who are living in California.

When they returned to the Philippines, Junior discovered their family property had been neglected for all the years after he left. It had become the city's open garbage dump accumulating ten tons of garbage daily, the buildings were squatted by some eight families.

Junior, on his own initiative, revived the family corporation and did what he could to save the family property. He made a promise to himself that he would do everything he could to preserve the family property so that all his siblings may benefit.

Junior traveled to Bataan despite the heavy rains, heat, typhoons and floods, and the chronic back pains he sustained from assisting his sister, Rosa, to move home. All by himself he packed, moved, unpacked and put his creativity into the interior design of her new massive home located on top of the mountain. The move required a 40-footer container which was filled with super heavy solid wood furniture, huge paintings, bronze statues, giant vases, clothing, boxes of documents and many other things. He is always willing to lend a helping hand to anyone and everyone.

Junior worked hard for several years to save and preserve the family property, and he did so with patience, perseverance and determination, not to mention financial expenses out of his own pocket.

EPISODE 14

DEMISE OF THE MATRIARCH

The Beauty of God's Sunset

"He will wipe every tear from their eyes. There will be no more death or mourning or crying or pain, for the old order of things has passed away."–Revelation 21:4

Two weeks before Thanksgiving in 1998, Consuelo bought her mother a long-sleeved silk dress with a close neck, green, white and black prints and an electric pleated skirt. The dress was the wrong size but Remedios loved it; they had a seamstress alter it to fit her. The dress was not quite ready when it came time to pick it up so Consuelo and Remedios spent the time waiting in the car talking. It brought back pleasant memories. Little did they know that the dress they were waiting for was the last dress Remedios would wear.

On November 26, 1998, Thanksgiving Day, as Remedios was getting herself ready for the party, she asked Rosa, "Do I look good with or without glasses?"

Rosa replied to her mother, "You look beautiful with or without them, Mama."

Remedios looked radiant, excited and ready for the Thanksgiving celebration. She looked forward to celebrating with her children.

When Rosa and Remedios were climbing the few short steps to go to the living room for the party, they were counting the steps, "One, two, three" … and four never came. Remedios fell like a limp rag doll. Rosa, who was the one holding onto her mother, could not catch her to prevent the fall. She felt so guilty and blamed herself.

The surgeon later told them that Remedios had suffered from a severe brainstem stroke. That was why she just fell. Her skull on the right side had caved in due to the fall, however, she did not die from the fall but from the massive stroke. She was flown to the nearby hospital but sadly never recovered consciousness, although she remained alive for a couple of hours.

While at the hospital and agonizing, at one point they could see tears flowing from their mother's eyes. It looked like she was in pain and still trying to hold on to dear life and did not want to leave her family. Eventually their youngest child, Jaime, lovingly and gently whispered to her, "It is ok Mama, you can go. You took excellent care of us. We are all grown and will be ok." Their oldest, Cecilia, said the same thing. As Remedios heard this, she took her one final breath.

Cecilia, Cesar, Rosa and Jaime surrounded her. Crispin, Teresa, Socorro and Junior were in the Philippines. Consuelo was at home and bedridden because she was sick at that time.

The son of Cecilia, gave a beautiful eulogy for Remedios:

"About nine or ten years ago, my grandmother was very disparaged, she turned to my mother, Cecilia, and asked her why she has not yet received the gift of tongues. My mother turned to her and then replied, 'you may not have the gift of tongues, BUT you have the gift of love, the gift of compassion and the gift of nurturing.' My grandmother then looked at my mother, speechless, very unaware of the positive attributes in which others saw in her. And that is one of her greatest gifts. She did not put on airs of conceit or self-awareness. Yet, anyone that encountered her was captivated by her presence and the depths of her being. She has the stature of a queen, the appearance of a first lady and always a demeanor filled with solemnity, dignity and, above all... grace.

There are many things that I, we, will all miss about her. Her spirit of charity. Her reverence to our Lord. Her love of the Sound of Music, sweets and closed necked blouses. Her smile, coupled with the words, 'join me' or my favorite: 'Yes my dear.' And, of course, her sense of humor.

I personally will miss her repeated story that most of you are familiar with. When I was six years old and a hemiplegic man walked into her house, I turned to her and asked, "Why is he dancing?" And for twenty years, she would recall that incident with so much fondness and laughter.

Yes, there are many things that we will all miss about her. Perhaps we may even have regrets pertaining to Mama; self-blame or faults we feel we may have committed. To that, I say offer it to the Lord. Pray for inner peace and above all realize that we have no faults when it comes to Mama. Everything is circumstantial without mal intentions. All of us in this room certainly wanted the best for her, and she knows that. Her heart is a vast ocean of love and understanding. That is the kind of woman that she was and that is the kind of woman that she still is, consumed with affection, up there looking down at us-all of us.

We are indeed many and a very tight, close-knit family. She would be so overwhelmed to see all of you here tonight, her family and friends. We are all here for her, as well as to comfort each other. And I'd like to speak for all when I tell Mama who is up there listening, "Please don't worry about us Mama. Coupled with your prayers for us, we'll be fine. You taught us well. You and Papa have raised eight children that you have showered with love, discipline, and dedication. You have sheltered your babies from danger, nourishing each one with only the integrity of your spirit, passion, and will. Although at times it may have been difficult and the atmosphere may have been dim, you persevered with tears shed resting solely on your faith in the Lord. From these eight children, you received eight more calling each one your OWN 'anak'. And of course, you were given eighteen grandchildren, one with a spouse, the other with a child. You loved us all with every ounce of fervent love that your body could possess. Oh yes, Mama, we'll be fine. You have done a superior job, unsurpassable. You give meaning to the word: Mother.

To her husband, our beloved Papa. I offer this advice, although this world may seem unrelenting, unbearable, take heart and do not focus on Mama's death, but on HER LIFE which will provide you comfort. You are now the rock of the family Papa, the sole proprietor. Be strong my endearing grandfather. Our benevolence for you has only increased at this time.

I'd like to close with one final story, occurring in the Philippines. I was about eight years old and I and all the little cousins, Joel, Jo-An, Coco, Margie, Ritchie, Allique, and Lyn-Lyn, would run outside into the courtyard whenever we saw or heard a plane fly overhead. Thinking it was Mama on the plane, we would all scream at the top of our lungs, 'Bye Mama! Bye Mama!' in hopes that she would hear us. Now all of us can do this, for she is up above and all around.

Bye Mama, our beautiful angel, our fragrant rose. You may, at last, retire into the heavens where you belong."

Remedios had a beautiful and solemn funeral service, all her children, relatives and friends attended and paid their last respects. She was interred at the Holy Cross Cemetery in Avondale, Arizona, where she would one day be joined in eternity by her husband, Crispin.

EPISODE 15

OUR LIVES WILL GO ON

The Busy Bees

"So whether you eat or drink or whatever you do, do it all for the glory of God."–1 Corinthians 10:31

In the year 2000, Crispin received PhP 85 million for unpaid legal fees from a bank that kept him as their legal counsel. He gave his partner PhP 40 million and used a portion of the money to buy more real estate properties, amounting to around PhP 10 million. After giving Teresa, Socorro and Junior half a million each, Crispin entrusted the rest of the money to his daughter Socorro, amounting to about PhP 30 million.

Junior continued taking care of their properties. He built perimeter fences, gates, and culverts, he had the lots re-surveyed for the precise technical details of the Transfer Certificate Title (TCT) for their Bataan properties. Together with Crispin, he also constructed a stunning home that was eventually known as the Farmhouse, he planted 100 mango trees, installed power and dug a deep well with an overhead tank. To achieve his goal, his strategies and plans required a lot of hard work and a huge amount of money, he did not ask for any help from his siblings even though they were in a better financial position.

He got a Tax Identification Number (TIN) for AMC and opened a bank account for the family corporation which had been dormant for twenty-eight years. This would allow the corporation to reopen for business as a holding corporation. He also paid all back estate taxes. Even though he did not have as much money as his other siblings, he found ways and means to save the properties and the family corporation.

While Junior was busy working to save the family properties, Socorro built a house for her family in Quezon City's elite neighborhood of Ayala Heights. It was a palatial home with magnificent features, modern appliances and the finest furniture money can buy. Every single item in the house was imported from the United States.

Socorro could also get the medications she needed to treat her Hepatitis C, which she got from a blood transfusion. The medication costs hundreds of thousands of pesos. Thankfully the medication helped her and eventually she was declared hepatitis C-free.

While Socorro and her family were preoccupied attending to the finer details of the construction of their new home, Junior continued to attend to the rigorous activities of the family properties in Bataan, requiring a few hours of travel each way, traveling in the wee hours of the morning to avoid traffic and coming back home by late afternoon.

Teresa remained busy with her governmental duties as a lawyer, serving her fellow men, minding her own business, oblivious to what was going on with the family properties.

In 2003, Cecilia was diagnosed with liver cancer and was given six months to live. She petitioned the Lord to extend her life and she received so many prayers from her family and friends. Her father flew all the way from the Philippines to pray for her. Crispin fasted for three days each time he prayed for Cecilia; he prayed for her for many days. Through God's mercy and divine intervention, Cecilia was miraculously healed. When she went back for a follow-up with her doctors, they were shocked that they could not see a trace of cancer. They could not believe it because all previous tests they had conducted showed positive for cancer. They tested and re-retested but no trace of cancer could be found.

EPISODE 16

ESTRANGED

Parting is Such Sweet Sorrow

"Honor your father and your mother, that your days may be long in the land that the Lord your God is giving you."–Exodus 20:12.

While Socorro's home was being built, she continued to live with her father in his house. Unfortunately Crispin and Socorro clashed once again. One early morning Socorro found out that her father had let a friend borrow her automobile, an old 1970 Toyota Corolla. She was enraged by this and confronted her father, berating him severely. The argument got heated. Socorro was told to stop by her cousin, who was present, but she persisted in her loud voice. Eventually Crispin went to his room. Crispin's chauffeur/bodyguard advised Socorro to leave before things get worse. Socorro did not want to leave and continued mouthing off in anger. Socorro, her husband and youngest son were led out of the house by their cousin.

Socorro called her sister Teresa to inform her of what had occurred. She asked Teresa if they could stay with her that night. Teresa said yes and asked her maid to prepare the beds for Socorro and her family. While Teresa was waiting for Socorro to arrive,

Crispin's maid called Teresa; she told her that Crispin was going to leave the house, alone, riding a tricycle in the middle of a storm. Upon hearing this, Teresa got so worried, rushed to her father to stop him and to console him. While Teresa was with her father, Socorro showed up at Teresa's house, because Teresa was not home Socorro presumed she was not welcome and left.

One day Socorro went to Junior's house, in her hand was a dried coconut husk supposedly with a bullet hole. She showed Junior and said, "look at the bullet hole. Papa tried to shoot me." Junior, who was disinterested, did not bother to look at it to examine what Socorro was showing him. This prompted Teresa to investigate what had exactly happened. She questioned the chauffeur who narrated to her what actually transpired… there was no shooting. He said he knew why their father went to his room; it was to get a gun. He knew that he would shoot his daughter--then shoot himself. That was why he told Socorro and her family to leave. "But there was no shooting." He reiterated.

The cousin was also questioned. She testified that there was no shooting at all. Teresa, being a lawyer and a former prosecutor, had many questions:

1. Papa is a sharpshooter. He can shoot flying chickens and will not miss. How did he miss Socorro?
2. If Socorro feared for her life, why did she go back to the ancestral home?

3.   If there was in fact a shooting, how did Socorro know the trajectory of the bullet and find where the bullet had landed, especially on a small piece of coconut husk?

4.   Where was the bullet casing?

Socorro abandoned her ninety-one-year-old father. She even stopped providing her father with necessities such as food. Upon learning of this sad predicament, the siblings in the United States sent money to support their father. The amount of money they sent was based on the list of expenses Socorro provided. Socorro told them she did not want to have anything to do with their father. The other siblings were heartbroken.

After more than a year, Crispin and Socorro reconciled, but sadly they got into another argument when Crispin asked Socorro for money. Crispin knew that Socorro still had the money that he had entrusted to her, after all, it was Php30 million and it cannot all be spent in just a couple of years. This, once again, enraged Socorro. She told one of her siblings, "So, the only reason he wanted to make amends was so that he could ask for money from me?"

It was around the year 2006 when Crispin and Socorro became totally estranged and never spoke to each other again. Crispin had been asking Teresa for years when he and Socorro could make amends. Socorro only had one response for Teresa, "It is not the right time." Teresa repeatedly relayed her father's message to

Socorro, but it fell on deaf ears. Crispin missed his daughter and loved her so much. His heart was full of sadness that could be seen in his eyes. Sometimes, even on recorded videos, the family could see tears flowing from their father's eyes.

Socorro's father was cared for by one maid in their ancestral home. Teresa often wondered if it was the maid, or Socorro, who decided everything for their father because she had to ask Socorro's permission every single time she wanted to visit. Nine out of ten times the answer would be the same… *"not the right time."* Teresa was always disappointed and crushed when she had prepared food to bring to her father but could not visit him.

While these things happened, that same year Junior continued to attend to their properties. After discovering Crispin had placed strangers on their Bataan property, Junior entered a ten-year lease agreement with a Korean church to be the land's caretaker. Pastor Kim spent over PhP 40 thousand reconnecting the electricity, clearing the vast land and performing routine maintenance when he took over the property. With permission from Junior, the pastor converted the house built on the property into a church. Junior always wanted to be of service to others and he was happy that most of the Filipinos who lived nearby could benefit from the church by having a place to worship.

EPISODE 17

PEBBLES IN OUR SHOES

It Never Ends

"I will instruct you and teach you in the way you should go; I will counsel you with my eye upon you."–Psalm 32:8

In 2009, the people with intentions of taking advantage of Crispin's generosity exerted efforts to convince him to hand over the titles to his properties. For easy read, we will refer to them as exploiters/inducers. It is worthy to note that these exploiters are the same people who surrounded Crispin whenever he was seen collecting money.

Crispin, not finding the Subdivision title in his filing cabinet in Matapat, filed an Affidavit of Loss with the Register of Deeds in Bataan. Perhaps he forgot that the Subdivision was in the name of Junior, hence Junior appeared before the Register of Deeds and showed the title with an Affidavit of Recovery. This put an end to the transaction.

To avoid more problems from the exploiters, in 2010 the siblings unanimously agreed to sell their 3-hectare Subdivision properties. In mid-2011, the said properties were sold and most of the proceeds were entrusted to Socorro. Also in 2010, another property under the name of AMC was sold. A buyer paid a little over PhP5 million for one lot, the proceeds of which were used to pay off all outstanding mortgages and other debts, including $30,000 owed to Rosa, she had once come to Crispin's aid to save a mortgaged property. First to be given the completed accounting settlement was Socorro in 2010. The shares were equally divided and five of the shares were entrusted to Socorro. However, years later, Socorro denied knowing anything--or of receiving any amount from the transaction☐-although she was the one who knew about Crispin's debts and informed all her siblings that they were paid off because of this sale.

Unrelenting, the exploiters continued to ask Crispin for other titles to his properties. He looked for the Farmhouse title but could not locate it. Junior later found out that their father filed an Affidavit of Loss for the said properties through a certain Michael Reyes who was unknown to Junior. As president of the AMC, he immediately filed an alternative Affidavit of Loss to safeguard the family properties. With two Affidavits of Loss being filed, the Register of Deeds elevated the issue to the Consulta; a quasi-judicial unit under the Land Registration Authority to determine which affidavit of loss should be honored. They decided in favor of Junior.

Despite the filing and annotation of an Affidavit of Loss and the favorable decision for Junior, a final resolution of the issue was not forthcoming. This is because Socorro refused to let go of the titles notwithstanding the fact that she and her husband signed an affidavit of loss of the titles in 2015. Socorro's husband even went to the Register of Deeds to present the 'lost' titles and later sent a letter addressed to the Register of Deeds admitting that she was in possession of the titles. Because of this, Junior filed a Petition for Mandamus, an extra special legal remedy. A (writ of) Mandamus is "a special civil action brought by an aggrieved party against a tribunal, corporation, board, officer or person unlawfully neglecting the performance of an act which the law specifically requires as a duty resulting from an office, trust or station." Per order of the Regional Trial Court, the petition filed by Junior was sufficient in form and substance and required Socorro to answer within thirty days. However, Socorro's lawyer requested an extension and was given another thirty days due to the reason that the case had only just been referred to counsel. Note that counsel belonged to an association of lawyers that handled a pending Estafa and Libel cases against Socorro filed several months before. At the time of writing, a judgement on both cases is still awaited.

EPISODE 18

SALE OF SUBDIVISION

Start of Schism

"And whatever you ask in prayer, you will receive, if you have faith."–Matthew 21:22

Given the siblings' difficult situation, they had no choice but to sell. It took some grueling deliberations via a series of teleconferencing among the siblings before it was finally agreed to put the Subdivision on the market.

Finally, on May 23, 2011, the subdivision was sold for PhP 30 million NET. The funds were divided into ten equal portions. Crispin had two shares and the remaining shares were divided equally among the eight siblings. Socorro was entrusted with the shares of Cecilia, Cesar and Consuelo, as well as Crispin's two shares for their father's needs. Excluded from the pooled entrusted monies was Socorro's share. Cesar and Consuelo told Socorro that she could spend their shares on Crispin, and that anything unspent should go to Junior. Teresa and Junior graciously accepted their portions. Rosa directed Socorro to set aside her share in case she needed it in the future, but she would eventually not take it and would ask Socorro to spend it on their father. Jaime gave Junior his share because he appreciated Junior's efforts and all the expenses he had incurred in saving the property.

Socorro didn't want their father to know about the money because she said if he found out he would demand it and might give it to his friends. The siblings agreed to Socorro's request to keep it from Crispin. While facing all these hard challenges, Socorro accused Junior of masterminding the sales of properties and that he made decisions about everything on his own without consulting the others.

EPISODE 19

KNOTTY SITUATION

The Spider's Web

"God is light and in Him there is no darkness at all."–1 John 1:5.

Crispin was led to believe that Junior kept all the money from the sale of their Subdivision and only gave each sibling PhP 1.1 million. This scheme was devised during a meeting between Socorro, Rosa and Jaime held at Socorro's residence. They told Junior to go to NY and hide there, to which Junior replied, "Why would I go there? What would I do there? What wrong have I done?" Junior did not want to leave his home and instead just hid from his father. He selflessly told them to just lay all the blame on him. He wanted to spare his siblings from any kind of problems, especially Socorro who had asked them all not to tell their father about the money, she did not want to be bothered by her father. Crispin was told that Junior fled to New York.

The family sold another property, called the Bridge, for a little over PhP 10 million in 2018, it was a property that originally had no access or pathway. This sale was transacted under Junior's name. He remitted to Socorro the full sum of PhP10 million, not a penny less. As usual, he provided a detailed account to each sibling, including a copy of the Deed of Absolute Sale. Socorro was happy as she continued to accept the funds entrusted to her. There were other properties sold, valued in the millions, before this one. Socorro received either a certain percentage of the money from the sale or, on some sales, she received the entire sum.

At the time of writing, Socorro, despite several demands, will not part with US$3.5 million in assets and funds. She has not liquidated, or produced accounts for, the monies entrusted to her for the care of their father.

Technically she only owns an eighth share of the properties, and as willed by their father, she has yet to relinquish the titles and is prepared to fight tooth and nail to keep all of them for herself.

EPISODE 20

DEMISE OF THE PATRIARCH

Pompeii's Pillar Stood Still

"He brought them out of darkness and the shadow of death and broke their chains in pieces."–Psalm 107:14

Crispin, a lawyer of sixty-seven unhappy years, grievously helpless against the Philippines' decadent moral and social values, a man of God with the spiritual gift of healing, and now overtaken by the darkening shadows of mortality, would no longer be aggressively fighting against the scoundrels. He just faded away peacefully with the heavenly splendor of the beautiful sunset beholding the spiritual glory of God.

Junior's phone rang at around 2:00 a.m. with the sad news from Socorro. Crispin was called home by God on January 4, 2020. Junior was devastated, but he was still able to think clearly, he coordinated with the funeral home that morning. He instructed Socorro to get funds for the funeral expenses from the money entrusted to her by her siblings, these expenses included first-class plane tickets to and from Arizona for Socorro's family considering her health and age. Junior reminded Socorro that there was more than enough money saved.

Socorro asked her siblings for another favor. She asked everyone to keep their father's death a secret. They did not notify any family member or friends. Socorro reasoned that Crispin's friends might appear. The relatives found out much too late and they all got upset as to why such important information, the demise of their beloved uncle, was kept from them.

Socorro called Teresa at around 3 a.m. to give the heartbreaking news. Teresa was inconsolable. She asked Socorro to pick them up because they didn't have a chauffeur. She wished to see her father at home and spend time with him, even if only for a few minutes.

At the first hour of business, Socorro rushed to attend to the funeral arrangements. Socorro had nothing to present when the funeral parlor asked for a death certificate so she went to the 'barangay' and told them what to declare on the death certification. Barangay is the smallest political unit of government in the Philippines. Each barangay is headed by a barangay captain and barangay council, each elected by the residents of the barangay.

Socorro told the barangay to put the cause of death as old age, pneumonia and multiple-site arthritis.

To Teresa's bewilderment, they were picked up late afternoon and taken straight to the morgue when their father was already embalmed. Beyond devastated, she wondered, *"Why the rush?"*

She also questioned in her mind, *"Papa was well and strong just a few days ago when I visited him, and now suddenly gone?"*

Later she learned that when Crispin's maid had called Socorro and told her that it seemed their father was no longer breathing, the first thing Socorro did was call Junior to ask for funeral directions. She did not consider sending a doctor to her father's house to check, or an ambulance to rush him to the hospital, or even a priest to administer his last rites.

It took three weeks to arrange and comply with all the documentation required before they could fly Crispin's remains to Arizona where he would join his beloved wife. The siblings in Arizona were surprised when they saw their father was just skin and bones--although still very handsome. In Consuelo's mind, she wondered, *"Why was he so thin? His skin was merely attached to his bones. Was he fed properly? Did he not want to eat for the few remaining years of his life? How could this once dashing, healthy-looking, man look like a skeleton?"* No one dared to ask for fear that they might offend Socorro who is often too sensitive; it is well-known that she could be easily upset and volatile so they wanted to avoid problems. Socorro volunteered some information in one of their meetings by saying, "He looked very skinny because he has been dead for three weeks."

While the siblings in Arizona were happy to see Socorro, the passing of their father deeply saddened them. Even though their dad was one hundred and three years-old, no one expected him to go, especially since no one had ever heard of any medical problems suffered by their father.

Consuelo was very distraught; she was scheduled to visit her father in February that year. She had created a beautiful photo montage video with her father's favorite music, it contained touching messages and captions. She had prepared gifts and was getting ready to go; sadly she was one month too late. Even to this day she regrets that she did not schedule her visit earlier.

A barrage of different emotions, reactions and coping mechanisms emerged from each member of the family, but each felt the same loss from the passing of their beloved father. They drew strength and encouragement from one another. They rehashed past stories and shared valuable lessons they had learned from their parents, this helped them grow their connections and guide each other along in this time of grief and healing. They were there for each other, as their parents would have wanted them to be.

Socorro, her husband and their oldest son transported Crispin's remains to the United States where he would be buried alongside his beloved wife. The siblings already in the United States gathered and met at Consuelo's house to plan the funeral. They decided who would be the pallbearers, the readers at mass, the church singers and the ushers. Jaime and his wife oversaw the flowers while

Consuelo and her husband oversaw the funeral home, the church and the cemetery arrangements. They had teamwork. A few grandchildren played a role in the mass celebration for their beloved grandfather.

The siblings all met with the funeral director to plan the perfect funeral service for their father. Crispin's beautiful prayer, written in 1978, was printed on a 2.75 x 3.75 laminated card and distributed to all who attended the viewing. The card featured an image of Jesus on one side and a small image of Crispin with the prayer that Crispin composed many years ago on the other side. It was written:

Merciful Lord God, our loving Father, hear our sincere prayer. Thanks, from the bottom of our hearts, for all Thy grace, mercy and love. Strengthen us to overcome our weaknesses and evil temptations. Let true humility, faith, charity and love reign in our hearts. We love Thee truly with all our hearts, mind and soul. Thy will be done with us and in all Thy creation always. Thine is the power, wisdom, glory, forever and ever. Amen.

Crispin gave this handwritten prayer to his children and asked them to pray it daily.

Close friends and family gathered to pay their respects at the funeral home. Consuelo and three grandchildren gave their eulogies, shared beautiful memories and important lessons they learned from Crispin. One grandchild, the youngest of Consuelo's family, shared her memory. It goes like this:

To many people, Crispin Reyes was a great and powerful man. Many know him as a war hero who fought in WW2. Others remember him as a fierce lawyer who fought against corrupt politicians in the Philippines, an endless job that never allowed him to retire. But to me, and to many of my cousins here today, he was our Papa. He was the man who loved me unconditionally, the man who taught me values that I still practice in my life today. Papa was my moral compass.

Papa taught me about living a healthy lifestyle. It is actually because of him that I feed my family green vegetables daily. It is also because of him I exercise regularly, and I made my children run triathlons when they were barely out of diapers. I remember as a 4-year-old in the Philippines, I would wake up in the early mornings at Matapat while the roosters were crowing, and the trees were still wet with the morning dew. Papa would be on the big white balcony doing his morning exercises without his shirt and his man boobs sticking out. I would join him, with hands on my hips.... inhale... exhale... repeat. To this day, exercise is a regular part of my life. It is a value that I have passed on not only to my children but also to the patients whom I care for every day.

Besides living a healthy lifestyle, Papa taught me one of the most important lessons in life.... to never be afraid. This was something he taught me over 20 years ago when I was applying to medical school. As many of you know, applying to medical school can be a grueling process. After completing 4 years of premed classes, taking my MCATs, completing my volunteer and research hours, and obtaining letters of recommendation, I was about to turn in my medical school application, then I stopped. I froze. I did not want to hand in my application. You see, I was scared. I was scared of rejection. I was scared that if I didn't become a doctor, then I would never make a difference in this world. Papa was visiting Arizona around that time, and somehow, he just knew. Many of us know about Papa's intuition. He was able to look at a person and know what was going on inside of them. And do you know what He said to me? He said, "don't be afraid. You are enough. God made you enough. Because God made you enough, you don't need anything else. You are enough to make a difference in this world. So, you don't need to be afraid". Because of this, I realized that while medical school was a vehicle to make a difference in people's lives, it was only just a vehicle, it is just a tool. Acceptance or rejection would not make me or break me. Because God made me, and therefore, I am enough.

I have carried Papa's lessons throughout my life. Today, when I've finished eating my green vegetables and doing my pushups, yet I still feel small, inadequate, just not good enough, I remember that I am God's work, and God's work is enough.

It's been over 20 years since I've had this conversation with Papa. I am now a mom, a wife, and a pediatrician. And I am grateful for the lessons that Papa has taught me.

I pray that whatever struggles, obstacles and insecurities you may have, that you remember that God also made you enough, and because you are enough, you do not need to be afraid."

They had a solemn and beautiful service for their father. People were touched and enthralled by the love and support that they saw among Crispin's children and grandchildren. Relatives and friends joined the burial procession the next day to say their last goodbyes. Every car on the opposite side of the road, who are not actually required to stop, saw the motorcade passing and came to a complete halt to show their respect. It was such a remarkable sight befitting a great man!

EPISODE 21

BITTERSWEET REUNION

Still United

"Blessed are those who mourn, for they will be comforted." - Matthew 5:4

Another meeting was scheduled at Consuelo's house to discuss other matters. Since they were already meeting, their brother Cesar asked if they could talk about their property in Bataan, not because he was interested but because he wanted to understand what was going on since he had been hearing a lot of problems about it, he was hoping he could help. Over the phone, Consuelo relayed this request to Socorro.

"Let us not have a meeting at all if we are going to discuss the property. I will walk out if it is mentioned" Socorro exclaimed angrily.

Consuelo was perplexed as to why Socorro became so irritated when this request was made, and why Socorro did not want it mentioned at all. They held the scheduled meeting but no one dared to mention the property. In another meeting, when Cesar mentioned the property Socorro said, "We do not need to talk about that."

Several topics were discussed during the meeting. Rosa, who is the most well-off among the siblings, suggested all siblings contribute to the expenses Socorro had incurred in the Philippines due to the funeral. Rosa also suggested that they give money to Crispin's maid. They gave $10,000 to Socorro and an additional $2,500 for the maid. Without mentioning that she still had money entrusted to her, she accepted the cash. Socorro never mentioned these monies to Teresa or Junior.

EPISODE 22

TO BE OR NOT TO BE

The Broken Glass

"Set your minds on things above, not on earthly things." - Colossians 3:2

Grief is one of the many human emotions. It is such a peculiar feeling because it does not always exist. The next thought may trigger a memory, allowing it to seep into your chest and anchor itself. Your heart feels like a brick dragging along the weight of sorrow and it sits there for a moment until happy memories flood your mind or something wonderful occurs, such as a child's birth, a wedding, a job promotion, or the simple joy of a bite of chocolate ice cream. Dopamine rushes can provide much-needed diversions.

The Reyes siblings experienced a roller-coaster ride of emotions in the aftermath of their father's death. They were all upset and wondered how he died.

On February 6, 2020, Cesar sent Junior an email in which he stated he thought the ancestral home in Matapat should go to Socorro because she lived there with her parents for many years and he believed she maintained it. He also said, in his opinion, the Bataan property should mostly, if not entirely, go to Junior because

Junior is the reason they still have that property. Further he said that Junior should be free to share it with Teresa and Socorro. Everyone agreed except for Socorro, who became angry upon hearing this and exclaimed, "Let us all go to court!"

The siblings continued to discuss the sale of their property, the Farmhouse. The AMC board of directors made a unanimous decision to sell this property on February 9, 2021 (AMC Board Resolution 02-09-21) authorizing Junior to do the negotiations of the sale. All five board members of AMC unanimously signed the Board Resolution which was witnessed, notarized and certified by the board's secretary. All siblings were furnished with the resolution, its minutes, the secretary certificate and the special power of attorney in his favor. This property has been on the market since 2010 but the decision to sell was renewed.

After the unanimous decision was made, and the Farmhouse was officially listed for sale, Socorro changed her mind. She informed Junior over the phone on June 9, 2021 about her plan to build a commercial complex on AMC's vacant lot; she even revealed to Junior that she had already visited China Bank to look into obtaining a loan to pay for the property's commercialization. Socorro explained that because of her son's mental illness he needed to be kept busy and this would be a great diversion for him. Junior advised Socorro to give the following options to the siblings:

1. Develop the properties into commercial use and if any of the siblings are interested to join they should have the option to do so.

2. Divide the property into eight equal parts and let each sibling decide autonomously for their share.

3. Allow each sibling to do whatever they want with their portion of the property.

4. Sell the whole as is, then divide the proceeds equally among the eight siblings as Crispin and Remedios had willed.

Socorro was not pleased with Junior's proposal, stating that, "The siblings in the US should not be included because they are all rich."

To which Junior replied, "That is not fair at all and all siblings have rights that need to be respected." Socorro's wish was obviously contrary to their parent's wish that the property be equally divided among their eight children.

Junior proposed to everyone if the building was turned into a commercial complex that a church be built on a small portion of the property with a landmark at the church's façade that displays, "In Memory of Crispin and Remedios Reyes." He wanted to have this church to continue serving as a place of worship for the Filipinos who live nearby. Except for Teresa and Consuelo, who would love to have those things built to remember their parents, no one supported Junior's proposal for whatever reasons they had. Junior also reminded his siblings that the undertaking of commercialization would take years and would everyone still be alive to benefit from its fruits?

One day, Socorro went to Bataan to visit the family properties. "Can you imagine being the owner and the pastor did not even acknowledge my presence?" Socorro complained to Junior in anger, "What if you were in my shoes? How would you feel?"

Junior replied, "It won't bother me at all." Junior, seeing that Socorro was not happy with the pastor who had been caring for the land for ten years, and seeing that Socorro wanted to take full control of the land, gave the pastor two months' notice to vacate the property. Socorro delegated responsibility for the land to the person whom Junior had previously paid PhP 200,000 to vacate the property which was fronting the so-called Bridge property. This was also the same person who Socorro had previously called a big liar. Why did she assign this 'liar' to be the caretaker then? Socorro even went to Teresa's house to ask if Teresa could draft a contract between her and the caretaker so that she would be able to evict the latter any time she wanted. Teresa vehemently refused.

Socorro had agreed in June 2021 that she would present Junior's proposals to the other siblings. She did not present the proposals by email but instead sent hard copies of the documents, four months later, purportedly on a note where Crispin had instructed that the properties should not be sold--this was despite Crispin's previous attempts to sell. Apparently, the plan being not to sell but to keep the properties as a "legacy". Cecilia received this note from Socorro and distributed it to everyone via USPS in November 2021. It was delivered with no explanation, leaving the siblings perplexed as to why they had received such a document.

Junior, who with hindsight, had learned a lesson from his previous transactions with Socorro, documented everything that occurred during his conversations and dealings with her, and distributed copies to all his siblings. Only then did the siblings realize why Socorro had sent them the document. Junior and Socorro clearly had had some unpleasant discussions about the property.

The siblings exchanged emails at all hours of the day and night. They were all stressed; some lost sleep over it, and the drama exacerbated some members' medical conditions. They drifted apart. Socorro referred to Cesar, Teresa, Consuelo and Junior as "your group" and to Cecilia, Rosa, Jaime and herself as "our group." They agreed, disagreed, argued and some proposed solutions to the problems, but all to no avail.

All the family members were saddened and hurt by the developing events. Hurting and being unhappy with one another are feelings frequently caused by how family members react to external events and to one another. People act against their better judgment and end up making terrible mistakes–sometimes because of misplaced, or change of, values along the way. But who doesn't make mistakes? What went wrong with this family?

EPISODE 23

THE FALLOUT

The Domino Effect

"Then he said to them, 'Watch out! Be on your guard against all kinds of greed; life does not consist in an abundance of possessions."–Luke 12:15

For months the siblings continued with their communications mostly through emails and sometimes phone calls. They were unpleasant emails, with some of them being hurtful. Cesar tried untiringly to solve their problem using all means of communications available to him. He was always a champion for the truth and what is right, and so wanted to unite the family and restore the peace.

On November 8, 2021, Jaime requested an accounting of all properties, all sales, the amount of each sale, who received the money and all jewelry with all supporting written documents. Junior sent everyone the accounts that he had previously given. Teresa, Cesar and Consuelo also provided some accounts. Cecilia, Rosa, Socorro and Jaime were those who did not provide the requested accounting up to the time of writing.

More antagonistic emails flowed and this prompted some members to ask about the most cherished ring that had belonged to Remedios. Teresa finally presented all the siblings with Remedios' handwritten letter, dated June 3, 1988, which had been sent to her and which she had kept all those years without showing to anyone. According to the letter Teresa was to receive Remedios' precious diamond ring, a set of other diamond rings and earrings, a large diamond cross and the money in the bank.

Consuelo began asking Rosa and Cecilia about the ring, she knew it was with Cecilia all along, but she just wanted to make sure and give her sister the benefit of the doubt. She asked Cecilia about it several times, but Cecilia denied having it. "I do not have the ring. I have no ring from Mama". She claimed.

After their mother died and when they discussed who should receive the ring, Socorro immediately stated that her mother said it should go to Cecilia.

Two weeks before their mother died, for some unknown reason, Consuelo was prompted to ask her mother, "To whom do you want to give your ring, Mama?"

Her mother replied, "Cecilia, your sister said it's for her." The phrase *"your sister said"* perplexed Consuelo. She did not, however, ask questions. Consuelo omitted this part and just told everyone when they asked that their mother wanted Cecilia to have it. She wanted to avoid problems so she kept it simple.

Teresa, being a lawyer, said, "Nothing can be more admissible in court than a holographic will. No amount of 'she said, he said' will prevail over a written will." A few of the family members denied Teresa the jewelry and the money, although a large sum of that money rightfully belonged to her. She was obviously beyond hurt, but it was not enough to allow anything… money, jewelry, or any other material things to come between her and her siblings.

Teresa said, "I will bring with me to life thereafter, my mother's love, and we will be together once more. I will kiss and hug you and say, I am sorry, Mama, for doubting your love for me. I was very wrong. Despite the doubts, one thing was certain: I love you every single day of my existence."

EPISODE 24

DESPERATE ATTEMPT

Divide and Conquer

"As for you, brothers, do not grow weary in doing good."–2 Thessalonians 2:13.

Several months from unanimously signing the AMC Board Resolution and Special Power of Attorney dated 02.09.21 to sell the properties, and after being told by Junior that they could realize hundreds of millions from the properties, Socorro emailed all siblings and vehemently denied signing the resolution. She also denied that both of her sons signed it as witnesses, even though all four of their signatures appeared on the documents along with all of the board members' attached government issued IDs, these were documents notarized and certified by the board secretary giving the special power of attorney in favor of Junior.

Although with legal documentary proof, still Socorro vehemently continued to deny the board resolution. On Saturday, November 20, 2021, 3:56 PM, Socorro wrote:

"Please be informed that we, (Jessy and Socorro), did NOT sign the Special Power of Attorney. Joel and Joseph (sons) did NOT sign as witnesses. The four of us (Del Prados) have not seen

Junior for at least five (5) years and on February 09, 2021, Jessy and Joseph went to a meeting at 9 am with the Barangay in Lubao, Pampanga.

Joel was with me (Socorro) when they went to this meeting so I would always have someone with me in case of anything as I had COVID.

Regarding the Board Resolution of Alliance Management Corporation of February 05, 2021, we (Jessy and Socorro) did NOT sign this board resolution authorizing the sale of Tuyo Farm.

Socorro

Everyone had had enough of the arguments. Nobody appears to agree on anything. Between Junior and Socorro, and later, Teresa, it grew into *"she said, he said."* Cesar was desperate to resolve issues and to restore the harmonious family relationship. He requested a meeting at Consuelo's house, which Cecilia, Rosa and Jaime reluctantly agreed to attend, but at least they showed up.

Cesar tried his best to explain to the family why the AMC Resolution dated 02-09-21 should be honored and followed. He said the documents were legal and binding. He explained how a corporation works. He printed copies of the board resolution and all the other documents which he distributed to them. Cecilia, Rosa and Jaime did not seem interested in the documents and they did not even want to look at them, at one point, Jaime cut Cesar off as he spoke and said, "Let's move on."

Cesar replied, "Can you please give me a chance to talk and to finish?"

Then Jaime asked, "Do you really want to know what I think about this board resolution?"

"Yes, what do you think?" replied Consuelo.

"I believe this board resolution is shit," Jaime responded. Cesar and Consuelo were shocked.

During the meeting, Consuelo called Teresa to ask if they all signed the board resolution. Teresa said, she will testify that they all signed. In fact, Teresa added, "Socorro was the one who brought all the documents to our home for us to sign." Jaime, Cecilia and Rosa, did not believe that the resolution was signed by Socorro, her husband and her two sons, despite Teresa saying she will testify to it. They did not say a single word when Teresa said this. Cesar's goal was sadly not met as the meeting ended. Cecilia, Rosa and Jaime did not take with them the printed materials which Cesar had given them in the hope that they would review at their leisure. They were not open to hear and find out the truth--their minds were closed.

Obviously, Cecilia's, Rosa's and Jaime's minds were already made up before they arrived at the meeting. They sided with

Socorro, supported her, believed her claim that none of her and her family had signed and they totally ignored the board resolution and all the documents which Junior had previously sent to all. No one bothered to call Junior to hear his side of the story. No one bothered to call Teresa to ask.

The adage that "money makes people do funny things" doesn't do justice to the actual problems and root causes of the family conflict. The combatants can always trace their problems back several years, if not all the way back to childhood. But what is it that so often drives people to wage war against their own flesh and blood over a loved one's estate? Is it even possible that one or more members of the family could have a partial, or full-blown, personality disorder that causes them to distort and escalate natural family rivalries into personal, and sometimes even legal, battles? Were there unsettled old grievances among them? Did anyone claim to have done a lion's share of the work in taking care of their aging parents and therefore assumed that he or she should receive most, if not all of the inheritance? Is there really a chance to dissuade them from provisions that are punitive, encourage them to mend fences while family members are still alive and leave a legacy of love?

Cesar, as determined as he was to resolve the family feud, tried several times to call, text and send documents via USPS, he also emailed Jaime, and Socorro's son Paul who is one of Socorro's advisers, and explained why everyone should honor the AMC Resolution dated 02-09-21. He was unrelenting. They all ignored him and he never heard from any of them. He also called Cecilia and Rosa and begged them to convince Socorro to do the right thing--but to no avail.

EPISODE 25

A MOUTHFUL OF GRAVEL

Sword of Damocles

"Whoever troubles his own household will inherit the wind, and the fool will be servant to the wise of heart."–Proverbs 11:29

On January 4, 2021, Socorro sent Teresa a four-page letter about the most precious ring that Remedios wanted Teresa to have. After sending Teresa the letter, Socorro painstakingly took the time to send the same letter individually to all her siblings. She claimed that their mother had changed her mind as to who should have the ring. Instead of simply saying why her mother supposedly changed her mind, she presented Teresa with a list of thirteen frivolous, malicious and libelous accusations. She annihilated Teresa's character and reputation by playing judge, juror, executioner and God. In her letter, absent of any evidentiary proof, she repeatedly used their dead parents' names. A small part of her email said:

"As years passed, she observed that you, Teresa, the values, morality, and compassion for your fellow man, honesty, and charity, slowly disappear. Those values they had given you were replaced with greed, indifference, deception, exploitation of others, and lack of compassion, not only for your fellow man, but for your family as well. She saw how you treated others because they were not as fortunate as you to have an education. You took the gift they gave you and turned it into something ugly. She too knew about most of the stories above and in the end, she simply changed her mind and decided and made 'habilin' (will) for the baguette ring would go to her eldest daughter (who she would normally stay with when she's in the States...) and someday be passed onto her wonderful daughter Lynn.

In the short time we have left on earth, I would advise you to spend your time repenting for your transgressions and making amends to those you have hurt."

Teresa was shocked beyond belief and suffered mental and emotional anguish from Socorro's vicious letter. She was heartbroken and suffered many sleepless nights due to the very hurtful and injurious letter. Everyone in the family couldn't believe what they have read; it was beyond shocking to read such a letter coming from a 'saintly' sister. Consuelo knew the true story behind some of Socorro's accusations against Teresa because she was a firsthand witness, but what would she do? Would she stand up for the truth, or just keep silent?

Socorro explicitly said in the same letter that Cecilia was in possession of the ring. She asserted that Cecilia had removed the ring from their mother's finger when she was in excruciating pain following the fall, at the time she was fighting for her life and surrounded by paramedics. She said, the ring was so tight that Cecilia had to remove it with soap. It is important to note that when this accident happened, their mother was in the USA while Socorro was in the Philippines--how did she know what happened that day? Cecilia's concern would have been for her mother's severe anguish rather than for the ring. According to protocol, everyone must stay out of the way of the paramedics while they treat and try to save a patient's life. Why would Cecilia be in the way when paramedics were working and trying to save their mother? Did this really happen? Cecilia, who previously and repeatedly denied that she had the ring, remained silent after Socorro sent this long letter to Teresa saying that Cecilia had it in her possession.

Teresa responded to Socorro's virulent email by saying:

"I was informed about your email from beginning to end– BEAUTIFUL AND ENTERTAINING. How rich can your evil mind get to concoct fictitious stories and lies while exalting yourself as a saint at the same time? You simply will never stop. A piece of advice - your genius in fiction can be better harnessed and

developed to the max inside the prison that is awaiting you. I can see two plausible scenarios. One, you can further develop being the number one master of lies while exalting yourself to the high heavens, or two, the prison can be a way to stop you from the continuous destruction of the solid reputation and integrity of others. Maybe, somehow, you might just realize behind bars all the evils you have been doing."

EPISODE 26

QUEST FOR TRUTH

He Said, She Said

"For what shall it profit a man, if he shall gain the whole world, and lose his own soul."–Mark 8:36

Consuelo, disturbed by the unfolding events, began going through her files. She also began looking for the ring (Remedios' grandmother's heirloom) that Socorro accused Teresa of borrowing and losing.

In Consuelo's quest for more information, she discovered a handwritten letter from Crispin, dated January 26, 1992, giving the ancestral home, Matapat, to Socorro, understandably, upon his death. It later transpired that she transferred the title in her name far earlier than her father had intended. In that same letter, Crispin also said that he wanted the Bataan properties divided equally among his eight children. Consuelo informed Teresa about it. Teresa, who was intrigued, investigated what had happened to their ancestral home. This ancestral home was owned by the family corporation. After some investigation, Teresa discovered that the property had been transferred to Socorro's name on February 8, 2005 while their father, who was then ninety-one years old, was still alive and well. Socorro kept this transfer from everyone, it came as a shock to all. How did Socorro do it when a title transfer under a corporation's name requires a board resolution or, even more so, a secretary certificate? Where was her conscience, taking the house her father was still living in? To the family, this was unimaginable, unconscionable and shocking. They just could not believe it had happened.

Junior emailed Socorro, with a copy sent to all siblings, about this discovery. As president of the family corporation he asked Socorro how she had transferred the ancestral home title into her and her spouse's names. In response to Junior's email, Socorro provided all siblings with the following documents: the title to the property in her name together with her spouse; their father's executed Deed of Absolute Assignment in favor of Socorro and her husband and a copy of a secretary certificate, signed by someone unknown, to all board members transferring the property to her name. Socorro did not present a board resolution document. The secretary certificate that she presented and used was signed by a stranger who was known only to her and her spouse. Socorro and her spouse are board members and so she definitely knew who the officials and directors of the board are and who should have signed.

A title transfer must have both a majority, or unanimous, board resolution and a secretary certificate which must be witnessed and notarized, otherwise everything is illegal. Although

Socorro is a board member and is aware that Teresa's spouse is the official board secretary, she used an executed secretary certificate signed by a stranger. "So again, how did you transfer the title to your name?" Junior asked.

It was at this point that Consuelo remembered her mother giving her an antique-looking ring, the ring Socorro accused Teresa of having borrowed and lost, so she went in search of it. She was surprised to find it in one of her jewelry boxes. She immediately informed everyone so they would know the ring had been found. Consuelo sent a picture of the ring to Junior and Teresa.

Emails between the siblings continued. Socorro deviated from the issues and emailed Junior questioning past sales since early 2000 the proceeds of which had been given/entrusted to her with detailed accounts and copies of all documents provided to all. "Is this where you did your hocus pocus, Captain Marvel?" Socorro asked Junior, referring to a specific property and sale. She added, "Junior is the mastermind behind all the sales.".

She was referring to Junior and accused him of stealing from the family. Weeks passed, Junior forwarded to all siblings the emails that he has previously sent to Socorro in 2010, they contained the accounting for the sale of the subject property. He sent this to Socorro almost immediately after the sale, although Socorro claimed she knew nothing about the sale, nor had she received any money from it. This is the particular sale of a property that was used to pay-off all of Crispin's loans and bank mortgages for the property where Socorro was living with her father. With all the accusations flying around things got even uglier, the family became more divided and some members suffered with health problems.

Socorro was obviously not addressing the issues at hand, she failed to answer where all the monies entrusted to her had gone, there were also outstanding questions about the accounts relating to a liquidation and the titles of properties that she would not let go of. Instead she went back in time and raised questions; she also made grievous accusations against Junior. She questioned all the previous sales even though she had already received a big share from some of those sales; in some other sales she was paid the entire sum--she gladly accepted the proceeds without question. If she had problems with the previous sales, why did she not ask at the time instead of waiting many years? The siblings who were on her side believed everything she said -- hook, line and sinker.

Consuelo's MS became exacerbated. She developed weaker extremities which meant she was now prone to falling everywhere, she developed blurred vision and was suffering from excruciating MS pains. The condition affected her heart and blood pressure and she was now having to rest in bed in between chores. Consuelo was forced to convert her bathroom into one with disabled access as she could see all this tremendous stress could eventually land her in a wheelchair. Even though this is what is happening to her, she accepts her fate wholeheartedly and braces herself for the worst when she can no longer walk. She said, "After all, with MS, I have had thirty-nine years of a good life, with mental acuity intact, able to talk, walk and do everything I needed, and wanted, to do. God is good."

EPISODE 27

IDEAL FAMILY SHATTERED

Not Who, But What Is Right

"If anyone says, 'I love God,' and hates his brother, he is a liar; for he who does not love his brother whom he has seen, cannot love God whom he has not seen."–1 John 4:20.

Although Socorro does not trust Junior, Junior makes it a point to consult and ask Socorro for her decision relating to all real estate sales of the family properties, he has done this for years and has always provided her with all the necessary accounting. It was convenient for Junior to talk to Socorro on Crispin's behalf because they both live at Matapat. With no intent or malice, Teresa was usually excluded since she lives in a different location and was always busy with work.

Whenever Socorro complained to Junior that there were just too many expenses at Matapat, Junior faithfully obliged and would hurriedly sell some properties that had been on the market for sale, the proceeds of which were always entirely entrusted to Socorro. Accounting was faithfully provided to all the other siblings together with all necessary supporting documents including copies of bank remittances and checks deposited under Socorro's name.

Socorro strongly opposed Junior negotiating the sale of their Farmhouse property because she accused Junior of deceiving the family in previous sales of family properties, despite her full knowledge of the transactions and with all the documents being provided to her almost immediately after each sale. She informed Cecilia, Rosa and Jaime of this, but they did not investigate or bother to ask, not even one query about Socorro's claims against him was ever heard. Socorro wanted to be the person in charge of selling the property. "Do you want a repeat performance?" she asked her siblings, referring to Junior and insinuating Junior had stolen from past sales. She was determined for others to believe in all her stories even though she had no evidentiary proof.

Teresa, Cesar and Consuelo believed that because of the board resolution, Junior should be the one to sell it. Junior had worked hard to keep the property so that his siblings could all benefit from it and he also wanted to fulfill the wishes of Crispin and Remedios. The family was split into two factions as divided by Socorro herself, one supporting Socorro's allegations against Junior, and the others who were supporting Junior. Cesar remained neutral, but because he did not back Socorro, she considered him to be an opponent. For convenience, we'll refer to Cesar, Teresa, Consuelo and Junior as Team A. Team B is composed of Cecilia, Rosa, Socorro and Jaime. They had teams which were equally divided which was sad but true. Socorro had successfully divided and alienated family members against each other--a strategy of divide and conquer.

Because of the unending arguments, accusations and counter allegations that ensued, everyone wanted to get rid of the property because it was causing a lot of animosity and pain, they just wanted to move on and close this chapter of their lives. Team B proposed they would get a third-party agent of their choice who would be under the direct supervision of Socorro, and Junior would only to be consulted should there be serious buyers. Socorro wanted to hold onto the titles and said that she wanted to be the one to hand the titles to the buyer. Socorro also demanded that when the property is sold, fifty percent of the amount of the check be issued to her and the other fifty percent to Junior. The email sent by Socorro to all siblings on February 11, 2022 stated:

We have talked amongst ourselves over the weekend and wanted to propose a solution that addresses your demand to surrender the titles to Junior. In lieu of your demand, Junior can sell the property, but under the following terms:

The four (4) titles will be kept with the four of us "Cecilia, Rosa, Socorro, Jaime" and which shall be turned over to the Buyer during the closing/final sale of transaction in exchange for the payment in the form of two (2) Manager's checks in equal amounts (totaling the Net Proceeds–see below), one Manager's Check payable to "Junior" or AMC and the other Manager's Check payable to Socorro.

xxx   *xxx*   *xxx*

Signed by all members of Team B

This did not sit well with Team A. They claimed Junior faithfully provided an accounting of all previous sales and documents, whereas Socorro had provided nothing--so, based on this, whom should they trust? They further claimed that by signing and agreeing to the board resolution, Socorro was grievously violating what was legal and binding. They also reminded everyone that if it were not for Junior, there would be no properties to talk about. Note that all four titles were held under Alliance Management Corporation (AMC) and the only person officially allowed to negotiate sales was Junior.

Other siblings may have forgotten that when the so-called Subdivision property was sold for PhP 30 million, Junior immediately provided the accounting to all siblings and remitted the entire proceeds of the sale to Socorro.

In the Philippines, unlike the United States, signatories and witnesses are not always required to appear before a notary public, this was particularly the case during the Covid pandemic, this became common practice. In fact, legal documents were delivered by a courier to the Notary Public's house. In previous negotiations, the AMC board members hardly ever met; they just talked on the phone amongst themselves. Once they agreed on a topic, Junior prepared all documents and sent them through a courier to Socorro and Teresa to sign, after which they would be returned to him. He would then get them notarized and he would send copies to all the siblings.

Socorro appeared to have forgotten this common practice and insisted that there was no AMC Resolution dated 02-09-21 because they had never attended a meeting in person regarding the sale of this property and they had never appeared before a notary public.

The AMC Resolution dated 02-09-21 happened at the height of the Covid pandemic. After Junior drafted the resolution, he sent it to Socorro for her and the other board members to sign. Socorro went to Teresa's house for her signature and the signature of Teresa's husband who is also a board member and acting as the AMC secretary. Socorro then sent the documents back to Junior so he could have them notarized. Because of the scary nature of the pandemic, the non-appearance of the affiants to the notary public was usually allowed given the special circumstances.

Junior brought the documents to a notary public who refused to notarize them even though they were signed by all board members, the reason given was because there were no witnesses.

Junior returned them to Socorro and requested the signatures of two witnesses. Socorro asked Junior who could be the witnesses; Junior suggested that since her two sons are of legal age they could both act as witnesses. Socorro had her two sons sign the documents and with government-issued IDs attached she returned them to Junior for notarization. Junior then returned to the notary public and the documents were finally notarized and copies provided for all siblings.

Socorro talked to Team B and once again vehemently denied signing the documents along with her husband and two sons. Team B believed her, whereas Team A believed in the board resolution and insisted on its implementation--the feud continued.

On February 12, 2022, Jaime wrote everyone an email pleading for an end to all the hurt and hoping to find an amicable and fair solution. He said, *"If you cannot find it in your hearts to find a peaceful and fair solution, I will never bother you again and this will be the very last time you will hear from me."* His previous proposal had actually favored their group and ignored the board resolution to which Group A did not agree.

Indeed, sadly, that was the last time anyone heard from Jaime. He went further and disconnected all members of Team A from his social media and even took down his recommendation for Consuelo's work on *LinkedIn* which is the world's largest professional network on the internet. One can use it to find the right job or internship, connect and strengthen professional relationships and learn the skills one needs for career success. Consuelo avails herself of the benefits of LinkedIn to find jobs for her photo montage video service. This is the same Jaime who always said, "There are always two sides to every coin."

Meanwhile, Junior kept trying to make people understand, he pleaded and begged, but all to no avail. Months passed and he gave Team B one last chance, he asked why they thought they weren't contributing to the problem by defending Socorro's accusations and demands. Rosa and Cecilia deviated, denied and rationalized, but they never inquired about Junior's side of the story. They never called Junior or Teresa to ask what had really happened.

EPISODE 28

UNIMAGINABLE

Love Unbound

"For what doth it profit a man, to gain the whole world, and forfeit his life?"–Mark 8:36

Beyond shocked and devastated by the unbelievable discovery, Team A could not believe their father's home had been taken from him without his, or anyone else's knowledge while he was still alive and well. Imagine that for sixteen long years Crispin was living in a house that no longer belonged to him because Socorro had already transferred the title to her name.

Teresa proposed to Socorro that she should reconvey ownership of the property back to the family corporation, Cesar also made the same suggestion. Junior offered to help to talk to Teresa, that should Socorro reconvey back the property to the family corporation, to legally transfer it back to Socorro and her spouse's names, but Socorro did not comply. Teresa couldn't just sit by and do nothing while a grievous crime was committed in the family by no less than one of the family members. Teresa drafted a reconveyance document in the simplest form and with words that would make for easy comprehension. Socorro could use this draft to work on the reconveyance of the property title which was her only option to avoid criminal prosecution. Teresa was serious about it. She said, "It is now your choice to decide either to get out of the issue quietly or go through the rigors of criminal proceedings."

Teresa felt compelled to right the wrong and to correct the injustice done to their father. It bothered her so much that she couldn't sleep for several nights. "Why take advantage of a 91-year-old?" she asked.

Teresa waited for Socorro and the rest of Team B to do something. Cesar pleaded with Socorro many times to reconvey and even stated that once it was reconveyed to the family corporation it could be legally returned to her. He wanted to avoid criminal proceedings, and worse, jail time for Socorro. "Everything would be done properly and legally." he said. His words fell on deaf ears.

Still, not wanting to give up, Cesar felt he must do what is right so he called Socorro. He wanted to plead to Socorro again to do the right thing. Socorro's husband answered the phone because Socorro was talking to Jaime on the other line. Cesar started by asking for a few minutes to say what he needed to say. Cesar started talking about the reconveyance when Socorro's husband got furious and began talking at the top of his voice so that Cesar could hardly understand most of what he was saying. One thing that Cesar clearly understood was when Socorro said, "You are all killing us, you are killing us." Towards the end of the conversation Cesar also clearly heard, Socorro's husband says, "Walanghiya" (shameless/ conscienceless). It is worth noting that this was not the only time Cesar tried to talk some sense to Socorro and her husband. At one point, after talking to them not only about their ancestral home but also about the Farmhouse titles, Socorro's husband said that they would discuss the matter with their son Paul and let Cesar know of their decision. Cesar never heard from them.

To keep everyone updated, Cesar emailed everyone and told them exactly what had been said during his conversation with Socorro's husband. Socorro replied to this email and boldly denied and said that it was not how the conversation went down. She said her husband was very calm and never uttered the word "walanghiya". Later it was discovered that while Cesar was talking to Socorro's husband, Jaime listened to the conversation on the other line.

In February 2022, because Teresa, having waited such a long time since she had last heard from Socorro or from any of the other Team B members, filed a legal case against Socorro, this is known as 'estafa through falsification of documents' which at the time of writing is awaiting resolution.

While Socorro extoled herself in front of her siblings, portraying herself as caring for everyone and protecting all properties from the clutches of 'dishonest' Junior, she was assassinating Junior's character and integrity. Will her emails really help her case or will they be used against her? Did she unknowingly provide Junior and Teresa with incriminating information against her?

EPISODE 29

FALL AFTER THE CROWN

Beyond Belief

"Then they will go away to eternal punishment, but the righteous to eternal life."–Matthew 25:46

Toxic resentment can sometimes arise from childhood dynamics. Sometimes awareness dawns that you have never liked the other person sitting at the dining table and you see no reason to keep trudging halfway across the country to see her. Sometimes an aging parent's needs, or the prospect of an inheritance, fires the burner under simmering dysfunction. What is really happening to this once beautiful and united family?

Teresa could not forget the four-page vicious letter Socorro had sent to her. If those words could kill, she would have died many times over. She couldn't understand how Socorro could think of all these unbelievable things to say about her, or how she could make up stories out of thin air. She kept wondering what was causing Socorro to act in this manner. Teresa, with her analytical mind, was curious and wanted to understand where Socorro was coming from.

Socorro was a sweet and quiet child, everyone saw her as a source of hope and inspiration. She was once regarded as being saintly, but eventually she was clearly exposed which undermined and destroyed the family. Socorro's mask has undoubtedly won over Team B. She knows how to swoon and speak in reassuring and encouraging velvety words that feel all too real; while her mind fantasizes about material obsessions resulting in the family division. She stayed for the long haul, patiently waiting until people's trust in her was almost complete. She patiently waited until both their parents had joined our Creator. Then, with an overly satisfied sneer, she pulled out the rug from under their feet, forgetting about the values, integrity and the importance of family relationships that had been instilled by Crispin and Remedios!

Now, Socorro's illusion has crumbled, exposing the rotten pulsating core she had kept hidden from the family for so many long years. Team A couldn't believe what she had done and what had happened to the loving family that Crispin and Remedios had raised. The parents must be turning in their graves.

Junior couldn't figure out what went wrong, or why he was accused of stealing when he and Socorro had always been partners in previous property sales. Junior did the legwork and Socorro's arms were always outstretched, palms opened, to readily accept the money with a sweet smile. Was it because Junior would not agree to her plans for them to develop the vacant property into a commercial complex, or to divide the land between the three of them while excluding their other five siblings? Was there really any plan at all for Socorro to share the properties with Teresa and Junior?

Teresa was desperate to figure out what had happened to Socorro. The only thing she could think of was that Socorro had always been envious of her because Teresa had accomplished far more than Socorro could ever accomplish in her life. Their father always talked to Teresa, consulted with Teresa--her husband was a partner in Crispin's law practice, they were always together, working together, eating together and sharing stories together. Teresa was also told by Socorro that she was the most beautiful and intelligent of the eight children. "You can wear any hairstyle because you are beautiful, unlike me, I would look queer with long hair." she told Teresa. Teresa was convinced that Socorro's web of lies, manipulation and deception resulted from greed and envy.

Teresa was most troubled by their father's final nine years. Despite their father's many requests for reconciliation with Socorro, they were immediately dismissed. When their father visited Socorro's house a few times, they never opened the door for him. Crispin went to see Socorro one last time but the guard at the gate, in an exclusive subdivision where Socorro lived, told him he could not set foot in the subdivision.

Teresa found all of this to be overwhelming and it devastated her. She also knew that their father's home had become a dumpster, with homeless people purposefully gathered at the front gate so that no one would dare go to see him, people wouldn't approach out of fear. No one, not even Teresa, could see her own father without permission from Socorro. Crispin was also deprived of phone use, the maid screened all calls, the doorbell was uninstalled and the cooling system was not turned on for him. "Papa was incommunicado" (cut-off from society), as Teresa put it.

On March 11, 2022, Teresa filed a legal complaint against Socorro and this time it was for libel because of the four-page libelous and malicious letter Socorro had sent to all. This letter was not only seen by the siblings and some of their spouses, but also by people outside of the family because Teresa had to seek help due to her health predicament. Socorro was fully aware of Teresa's physical challenges. In the Philippines, the publication as a requirement for libel had already been expunged by jurisprudence to include the defamatory statement reaching people other than the addressee. They are still awaiting the resolution of this complaint.

Will Socorro face more new legal proceedings from the quiet, unselfish, self-sacrificing Junior? Will he just make his move when he thinks it is time to checkmate and shock Socorro? Or will he just let all these matters pass and remain in silence?

Working through, resolving, releasing and forgiving a family member who has hurt you beyond repair, even if you have no contact with them, appears to be impossible. Or is it? Even if the unfathomable grief may pass, the extremely deep scars would last for a lifetime.

EPISODE 30

ABSENT PEACE

Queries Hanging on a Thread

"And he said, 'Hear my words: If there is a prophet among you, I the Lord make myself known to him in a vision; I speak with him in a dream.'–Numbers 12:6

In the Reyes family, there are a few members gifted with visions in their sleep. One of them is Consuelo. She has seen so much in her dreams that she sometimes wishes that she did not, especially when the dreams are emotionally disturbing. She has seen accidents, births in the family, weddings and the death of family members and friends who have died or would soon die.

In Consuelo's recurrent dream, the big old house was dark and there was a bed in a tiny room which was darker than the rest of the house. On the bed Crispin was curled up in a fetal position, he was sick, weak and unable to move, all was deafeningly silent. In a faint voice Crispin uttered, "Please forgive me, from now on I will be a good boy." He said this as a lady standing by the bedside was castigating him, one hand on her waist, the other hand up in the air with her forefinger angrily pointing at him. Consuelo has seen this dream countless times. It bothered her but she did not know what it meant. She eventually asked Teresa to investigate.

Teresa became concerned and obliged. Teresa could not elicit any information from her father after questioning him.

In 2022, Consuelo contacted Socorro's son, Joel, to find out how they were all doing. The conversation led to Consuelo asking about their ancestral home. Joel told her that the large items like the furniture were being taken to their property in Bataan which was the property on the market for sale, the rest of the things were being taken to Socorro's house. Socorro never even bothered to ask any of the siblings if they would like to have any memento from their parents that they could treasure. She also planned to just donate all of Crispin's lawbooks to some charity instead of giving them to Teresa who had been wanting to have them. Consuelo was perplexed, thinking, why take the furniture there when it is to be sold? So she asked Joel what their mother was planning to do to Matapat. He replied,

"We are planning to fix it because the house is totally unlivable. The roof has holes and is rotten, electrical wires are broken, wires are exposed, the entire house has termites, roots grow around water pipes, pipes leaking, toilets and drainage are clogged, lights fell, and the gate is full of rust."

This news astounded Consuelo. Socorro was entrusted PhP 35 million by their father in 2000. Her siblings entrusted her with another PhP 17 million in 2011; another PhP 10 million in 2018, besides several millions from the sale of other properties. Crispin lived for nine years after she was given PhP 17 million from the sale of their Subdivision plus another PhP 10 million. Consuelo wondered how the house could have deteriorated to this state as described by Socorro's son, she wondered if Socorro's claim that she had spent all the money on Matapat's maintenance and repairs was true. When asked about the money entrusted to her, Socorro stated, "There were so many expenses. I must maintain our father's reputation as a prominent lawyer and keep his high social standing."

According to Consuelo's husband, a professional structural engineer, the money entrusted to Socorro was more than enough to build another palatial home in an affluent neighborhood like the one Socorro lived in, together with all the expensive furniture and appliances required, and there would still be a lot left over. Socorro had also claimed that their father asked her for hundreds of thousands of pesos, how did that happen when they had absolutely no contact at all for approximately thirteen years before he died? She has been hiding from her father, saying, "He will just ask for money." How could she claim she maintained and repaired the ancestral home if the condition was what her own son, Joel, had described? It was the description of the house by Joel that triggered Consuelo's curiosity. She googled the street-view of the house and the pictures she saw shocked her. The pictures showed all the way back to 2014. She could not believe her own eyes, it was definitely not a house appropriate for a prominent lawyer, not even for ordinary people. It simply looked like an open garbage dump. "How could anyone bear this? How could Socorro bear living in such an elite neighborhood, living luxuriously, while her own father lived in a garbage dump?" Consuelo, in tears, asked with disgust.

Many questions remained unanswered for several family members. One of the many questions was why Socorro did not call a doctor or ambulance and send them to their father's house to check on him when she was told he was no longer breathing? Instead Socorro's focus was on the funeral arrangements and she immediately called Junior to ask for funeral information. Why was Teresa, who was called at 3:00 am, not picked up until late afternoon and then driven straight to the morgue when she had specifically requested to be picked up so that she could see her father at home and spend a few minutes with him? What was the rush? Why didn't Socorro explain to her siblings how their father had died? Wouldn't that be a given and need not be asked? Unfortunately they have so many questions to which they will never find the answers.

Consuelo continued to see her father in her dreams, sad and silent. Consuelo's father has now been gone for almost three years, but he still appears. What exactly does this mean? Could it all be related to what's going on within the family, or does Crispin want the family to know what went on during his last few years of life?

Consider a world in which no one desired what belonged to others, where children honored their father and mother, where the family unit thrived in love and peace and where people obeyed the commandments not to lie and steal. Wouldn't Crispin and Remedios be happy observing their children from heaven? Wouldn't we have a better world to live in?

EPISODE 31

NO TWO PEOPLE ARE ALIKE

Easier To Forgive Than to Forget

" "You, Lord, are forgiving and good, abounding in love to all who call to you." -Psalm 86-5

No two branches of a tree are alike, just like a signature, a thumbprint, DNA or the pupil of an eye. The branches grew and grafted into different places, the leaves changed shape, size and color, completing a magnificent cycle and unique form. Each of its natural growths, combined with the warmth of the weather and the seasonal rain, reaps graces sent from above, far beyond anything anyone could ask for. The heavens never once overlooked the beauty of HIS creation, even during storms and drought. After every storm, the sun rises.

Our lives' puzzle pieces will eventually fall into place, completing a beautiful art of life's journey. We are writing our own stories and painting our own landscapes every moment of our lives. How will the books of the Reyes siblings be read and how will their painting be completed? Only God and those of us who are true to ourselves would know the paramount of truth while God has allowed us to live in this borrowed forsaken world.

As we all know, no one is exempt from being hurt. The most painful hurt we suffer from is caused by our loved ones. Sometimes it is God's way of trying to communicate to us, to tell us He is always here present in our lives, waiting for us to talk to Him. But if we stay focused on God, it will help us overcome the difficulties in life, no matter how excruciatingly painful the hurt is.

With God's infinite mercy and unceasing love for all of us, when the pain inflicted upon us is unbearable, God will help us know ourselves and will lead us to the right path we need to take rather than feel depressed, hate or, in most cases, get angry and become vengeful. It is important to never cease to pray. During those testing times we need to fix our gaze on God.

It could take a long time for us to forgive. Forgiveness is not for the offender alone, but also for the afflicted. Forgiveness releases the afflicted from pain. It may mean reconciliation, but sometimes it means letting go of the aggressor. With the grace of God, no matter how painful the transgression was, forgiveness is possible. We may have a hard time forgetting the pain, but we can always forgive. One's motivation should not be based on what we may not get, but on the positive things and change we can do. It is not a matter of who is right, but what is right under the eyes of our Lord. We may be used as a tool to right the wrong but that should be done under the laws of men and the laws of God. Will the Reyes brothers and sisters be able to forgive? Who would have guessed that a family whose lives began with so much love could end up in such unimaginable pain?

EPISODE 32

THE DARK TWILIGHT

Not Even God Will Turn Back Time

"In the twilight, in the evening, in the black and dark night,"– Proverbs 7:9

The Reyes family is in the autumn of their lives. Cecilia is the oldest at 86 years old, followed by Cesar at 83, Teresa at 79, Rosa at 77, Consuelo at 75, Socorro at 73, Junior at 70 and Jaime at 68. No one would have expected that from childhood, after decades of beautiful, loving, harmonious relationships, they would have reached this point of almost no return. Trust is earned over the years, and once lost, it takes a miracle to gain it back. The siblings have lost the trust and respect for one another. What could be their only saving grace to gain back the once loving and united family? Where are they now?

Cecilia has encountered many dangers and hardships in life. She survived them all only through the help, mercy, grace, protection and love of God. Despite experiencing hurt and sorrow, she always followed her own words: "BE NICE AT ALL TIMES, it will not cost you anything." Throughout Cecilia's life, she experienced the loss of many friends and loved ones. Yet even after facing her own mortality, she does not have a fear of death. She grounded her fearless connection to dying in her relationship with God. Knowing Him provides her with solace and her fear dissipates based on her relationship with Him.

God blessed her with two beautiful children. Her son lives in Burbank, California. He earned a Bachelor of Science degree in journalism. Her daughter lives in Phoenix, Arizona, she is married. She earned a Bachelor of Science degree in biomedical engineering. Cecilia earned a Bachelor of Science degree in pharmacy and medical technology. She lives in Glendale, Arizona with her husband and enjoys being retired. She is blessed with one grandson.

Cesar continues to suffer from asthma and willingly offers his suffering to God. He busies himself helping family members with their financial investments. He has twenty-nine years of experience in that field and he is good at what he does. He was blessed with two children. His daughter is married and lives in California. She earned a bachelor's and a master's degree in cell biology. His son, who is single, also lives in California. He earned his degree in journalism. Cesar earned a bachelor's degree in management. He has two grandchildren. He and his wife live in Glendale, Arizona and are enjoying retirement.

Teresa earned a Juris Doctor degree, with cum laude honors and is a retired distinguished lawyer in the Philippines. She has dedicated her life to fighting for justice. A kind and sincere heart matched her boldness with a fearless spirit. She is fair, just and upholds the truth. Teresa has a solid and sterling reputation among her colleagues in the Philippines. She cannot be bought. Big companies and corporations gave her blank checks to do as she pleased--but to no avail. Just like her father, she has occupied important government positions. Teresa's outstanding reputation extends to foreign countries. They sent Teresa as a Philippine delegate to the Geneva Convention in Switzerland and to the Vienna Convention in Austria. People gave her a standing ovation for her powerful and outstanding performance. Though small in stature she commands respect. Teresa has done so much good for humankind and won all the cases and causes she has overseen, improving countless lives in the Philippines.

Sadly, Teresa lost her sight in 2014. Though faced with a difficult predicament, she enjoys and provides legal aid to those in need. She occupies her time with prayers and playing the piano.

She has a son and a daughter who both earned a bachelor's degree in business administration. Teresa has two lovely grandchildren who are both gifted in music. She lives in the Philippines with her husband who is almost blind because of a brain hemorrhage.

Rosa and her family left New York many years ago and moved to Arizona. She had a thriving practice in pediatrics for almost forty years, that ended because of health reasons in 2011. Even though she has retired, she loves to offer medical care to those who need it. She enjoys medicine and learning new things every day. She likewise enjoys accompanying others to their doctor's appointments because by doing so, not only is she able to help, but she continues to learn new things from different specialty doctors.

Rosa has two children. One earned a bachelor's degree in medical technology and the other son earned a degree in medicine. She is blessed with three grandchildren. She enjoys retirement with her husband and lives in Glendale, Arizona.

Consuelo is a perfectionist and lives with OCD in most things, she loves to create photo montage videos accompanied with music. Her artistic skills are excellent. She founded Creative Artistry Photo Montage Videos based in Phoenix, Arizona. Blessed with creativity, she founded, and was the co-owner of, Precious and Few, floral arrangements also based in Phoenix, Arizona. Countless people rely on her help with computer issues, resume writing, application letters and letter of recommendations among other things. Her fascination with technology is driven by its fast-paced progress. She can build a computer from scratch. She enjoys floral arrangements and makes sure that her parents always have beautifully designed flowers.

Consuelo has been afflicted with Multiple Sclerosis (MS) since 1983. In multiple sclerosis, the protective coating on nerve fibers (myelin) is damaged and may eventually be totally destroyed. Depending on where the nerve damage occurs, MS can affect vision, speech, sensation, coordination, movement, mental acuity, bladder and bowel control and the patient, towards the end, becomes a vegetable. MS has not stopped her from doing the things she loves to do. She has three children. Her oldest child earned a bachelor's degree in nursing, her second child earned an associate degree in clinical laboratory science and her youngest holds a degree in medicine. Consuelo earned a bachelor's degree in business administration. Her eight grandchildren enjoy visiting her in Glendale, Arizona, where she lives with her husband.

Socorro had two life-threatening incidents. When she was several months pregnant, she was not aware that the child did not have a heartbeat. The doctor knew the fetus had no life but waited weeks before they did the surgery and she almost lost her life. She hemorrhaged and needed a blood transfusion. She was infected with hepatitis C because of the blood they gave her. Because of this, she suffered from chronic fatigue because of liver damage. Modern medicine saved her just in time before she had liver failure. The second time, she nearly lost her life was to Covid-19 in 2021. They gave her a 50/50 chance to live, and with humility, she asked forgiveness from everyone whom she may have wronged. Obviously, she still has a mission on Earth--but it seems she is back on her old hamster wheel.

Socorro lived with her parents for 26 years until she built her own home in Ayala Heights. She has three sons. The oldest earned a bachelor's degree in management, the second has a degree in medicine and the third has a degree in entrepreneurship. Socorro earned a degree in accounting. She lives in the Philippines with her husband and two sons. She has no grandchildren.

Junior did not hold an ounce of anger or bitterness in his heart. *"So fragile is our heart that of all the human organs, there is only one sacred–heart"*. The invisible, though healed scars, with varying width, length and depth, stayed within his persona. His hands and feet would show the shadows of those years. Only God knows why Remedios' confidant brainwashed her into believing that Junior was the black sheep of the family when it was farthest from the truth. With all of Junior's past hardships in life, he continues to stand tall and courageous, remaining true to himself, his family and others. He said his purpose in life is to serve and live for others.

He has two children. One has a bachelor's degree in journalism and a master's in public health and the other has a bachelor's degree in design studies. He is blessed with four lovely grandchildren. Junior earned a bachelor's degree in architecture. He spends his time helping his community and is active in several charitable organizations, also sending some youngsters to school and all the way to college. Just like his father, who loved nature and all the creations of the Lord, he enjoys his garden, fishpond, plants, trees and living a simple life with his wife in the Philippines.

Jaime still works part-time for American Express as lead project manager as of this writing. He busies himself with all kinds of projects in his home undertaking never-ending upgrades and renovations. He has two children who both earned a bachelor's degree in teaching. Jaime earned a bachelor's degree in economics and computer science. He has four grandchildren. He lives in Glendale, Arizona with his wife.

Teresa, Socorro and Junior live in the Philippines, not too far from each other. Cecilia, Cesar, Rosa, Consuelo and Jaime live within a 2-mile radius of each other in Glendale, Arizona.

Each member of the family has been affected and the severity of their ailments has progressed in varying degrees. They were crushed by their shocking discovery and even more so by the division of the once loving and united family. Everyone was blind to the years of deception that is why, to them, all these events are beyond belief. They still find it hard to comprehend how one 'saintly' family member could harm her own flesh and blood.

Team B was completely blinded by Socorro's mask and could not see past it. Who can blame them after so much brainwashing for so many years? Like a fragile crystal, the family was instantly shattered into a million little pieces.

Despite the unbelievable discoveries and the bitter feelings, maybe, just maybe, this broken family will be able to once again be unified, to love and support one another despite their belief that these traumatic truths cannot be rectified, reversed, or forgotten. The ideal family that Remedios and Crispin worked so hard to build, and made so many sacrifices for, could then revert to being what they were used to being. They may all agree that there is no turning back at this point and that the harmony lost will never be recovered. Will they be able to rekindle their love, trust, respect and support for one another? Is it at all possible after the trust has been broken? It really seems impossible. Who can say for sure?

Jesus said to them, *"With man, this is impossible, but with God, all things are possible."* 19:26 -Matthew

"The most painful tears are not the ones that fall from your eyes and cover your face. They're the ones that fall from your heart and cover your soul." – Author Unknown

www.ingramcontent.com/pod-product-compliance
Lightning Source LLC
Chambersburg PA
CBHW020959160726
47994CB00006B/2300